D1719631

STARK

Original-Prüfungsaufgaben
mit Lösungen

MITTLERER SCHULABSCHLUSS

Englisch 10. Klasse

Nordrhein-Westfalen

2010–2017

MP3-CD

STARK

© 2017 Stark Verlag GmbH
8. ergänzte Auflage
www.stark-verlag.de

Inhalt

Vorwort

Hinweise zur zentralen Prüfung am Ende der Klasse 10

Kurzgrammatik

Original-Aufgaben der zentralen Prüfung

MP3-CD

Die Hintergrundgeräusche auf der CD stammen aus folgenden Quellen: Pacdv, Partners in Rhyme, Freesound und Soundsnap.

Jeweils zu Beginn des neuen Schuljahres erscheinen die neuen Ausgaben der Abschlussprüfungsaufgaben mit Lösungen.

Autor

Martin Paeslack: Lösungen zu den Prüfungsaufgaben
Kurzgrammatik: Redaktion

Vorwort

Liebe Schülerin, lieber Schüler,

dieses Buch enthält die **Original-Aufgaben** der zentralen Prüfung **der Jahre 2010 bis 2017** zur intensiven Vorbereitung auf den **Mittleren Schulabschluss 2018**. Es ist insbesondere für die **Vorbereitungsphase unmittelbar vor der Abschlussprüfung** gedacht und hilft dir dabei, noch mehr Sicherheit im Umgang mit Prüfungsaufgaben zu gewinnen.

Mithilfe der Original-Prüfungsaufgaben kannst du testen, ob du für den „Ernstfall" gut gerüstet bist. Versuche, eine komplette Aufgabe in 120 Minuten zu bearbeiten – diese Zeit steht dir auch in der Prüfung zur Verfügung. Kontrolliere erst danach deine Lösungen. Hast du viele Fehler gemacht bzw. hat dir die vorgegebene Zeit nicht ausgereicht, arbeite die Aufgaben noch einmal durch. Wenn du nur sehr wenige oder gar keine Fehler gemacht hast, kannst du ganz entspannt in die Prüfung gehen.

Die beiliegende **MP3-CD** enthält die Hörverstehenstexte der Original-Prüfungen. Sie hilft dir dabei, dein Hörverständnis gezielt zu verbessern.

In der **Kurzgrammatik** werden alle wichtigen grammatischen Themen knapp erläutert und an Beispielsätzen veranschaulicht. Hier kannst du nachschlagen, wenn du in der Grammatik einmal unsicher sein solltest.

Der Band „**Training Mittlerer Schulabschluss 2018**" (Best.-Nr. 51550 bzw. 51550ML mit digitalem Prüfungstraining) bietet dir weiterführende Übungsmöglichkeiten. Er enthält neben den Original-Prüfungen 2016 und 2017 zahlreiche Übungsaufgaben zu allen prüfungsrelevanten Kompetenzbereichen. Darüber hinaus werden dir Strategien zur effektiven Bearbeitung der Aufgaben vermittelt. So kannst du deine sprachlichen Fertigkeiten gezielt trainieren und dich langfristig auf den Mittleren Schulabschluss vorbereiten. Arbeitest du gerne am PC oder Tablet? Dann empfehle ich dir die Ausgabe mit digitalem Training.

Sollten nach Erscheinen dieses Bandes noch wichtige Änderungen in der zentralen Prüfung 2018 vom Ministerium für Schule und Weiterbildung bekannt gegeben werden, findest du aktuelle Informationen dazu im Internet unter: http://www.stark-verlag.de/pruefung-aktuell

Viel Spaß beim Üben und viel Erfolg in der Prüfung!

Martin Paeslack

Hinweise zur zentralen Prüfung am Ende der Klasse 10

Im Schuljahr 2017/2018 finden die zentralen Prüfungen zum Erwerb des Hauptschulabschlusses nach Klasse 10 oder des Mittleren Schulabschlusses (Fachoberschulreife) an folgenden **Terminen** statt:

	Haupttermine:	Nachschreibtermine:
Deutsch	08. Mai 2018	29. Mai 2018
Englisch	15. Mai 2018	05. Juni 2018
Mathematik	17. Mai 2018	07. Juni 2018

Bearbeitungszeit
Die Bearbeitungszeiten für die schriftlichen Prüfungen wurden vom Schulministerium folgendermaßen festgelegt:

Deutsch	150 Minuten
Englisch	120 Minuten (40 Minuten Teil 1, 80 Minuten Teil 2)
Mathematik	120 Minuten

Darüber hinaus werden in allen Prüfungsfächern 10 Minuten zur ersten Orientierung gewährt (Bonuszeit). Diese können entweder einem der beiden Prüfungsteile zugerechnet oder auf beide Teile aufgeteilt werden. Solltest du mit dem ersten Prüfungsteil schon vor Ablauf der zur Verfügung stehenden Zeit fertig werden, darfst du sofort mit dem zweiten Prüfungsteil beginnen.

Ablauf der schriftlichen Prüfung
Die schriftliche Prüfung im Fach Englisch besteht aus zwei Teilen:
- Im **ersten Teil** werden die in den Klassen 5 bis 10 entwickelten **Basiskompetenzen** im Bereich **Hörverstehen** und **Leseverstehen** überprüft. Sie sind – unabhängig von der Schulform – identisch für alle Schülerinnen und Schüler, die auf demselben Abschlussniveau geprüft werden.
- Im **zweiten Teil** der schriftlichen Prüfung werden Aufgaben gestellt, die **Kompetenzen aus den Jahrgangsstufen 9 und 10** voraussetzen und sich auf die inhaltlichen Schwerpunkte beziehen. Die hier abgeprüften Bereiche sind **Schreiben** sowie die **Verfügbarkeit sprachlicher Mittel und sprachliche Korrektheit** (d. h. variierende Aufgabenformate zur Überprüfung von Inhaltswörtern, häufig verwendeten Kollokationen und funktionalen Strukturen).

Schwerpunktthema

Für die kommende Prüfung wurden **Großbritannien** und **Südafrika** als Bezugskulturen ausgewählt. Du wirst also Aufgaben erhalten, die mit diesen beiden Bereichen etwas zu tun haben. Dabei musst du eventuell Informationen heraussuchen und neu zusammenstellen oder Vergleiche mit Deutschland anstellen.

Es ist also sehr hilfreich, wenn du dich vorab über Großbritannien und Südafrika informierst. Du kannst z. B. im Internet recherchieren oder eine themenbezogene interessante Dokumentation im Fernsehen ansehen. Je mehr Hintergrundwissen du dir vorab angeeignet hast, desto leichter wird es dir fallen, die entsprechenden Aufgaben in der zentralen Prüfung zu lösen.

Noten

Deine Abschlussnote setzt sich aus der Prüfungsnote als Ergebnis deiner schriftlichen Prüfung und der Vornote zusammen. Diese Note beruht auf **all** deinen Leistungen seit Beginn des Schuljahres. Auch Hausaufgaben, mündliche Leistungen, Mitarbeit, Heftführung, Referate und Gruppenarbeitsergebnisse zählen zu diesen Leistungen.

– Stimmen Vornote und Prüfungsnote überein, ist die Vornote auch die Abschlussnote. Bei einer Abweichung von einer Note entscheidet dein Fachlehrer zwischen beiden Noten.
– Falls Vornote und Prüfungsnote um zwei Noten voneinander abweichen, kannst du dich einer freiwilligen mündlichen Prüfung im Fach Englisch unterziehen. Falls du das nicht möchtest, wird der Mittelwert aus Vornote und Prüfungsnote gebildet. Du solltest aber unbedingt mit deinem Fachlehrer deine Situation besprechen und klären, ob es sinnvoll ist, sich für die mündliche Prüfung anzumelden.
– Weicht deine Prüfungsnote um mehr als zwei Notenstufen von der Vornote ab, ist die mündliche Prüfung für dich verpflichtend.
– Die mündliche Prüfung findet zwischen dem 25. Juni und 3. Juli 2018 statt.

Die Bewertung deiner schriftlichen Prüfung erfolgt durch die Vergabe von Punkten. Den Arbeiten wird eine Tabelle zur Umrechnung der Punktwerte in Noten beigefügt. Dabei werden der erste und zweite Teil entsprechend der vorgesehenen Bearbeitungsdauer gewichtet.

Grundsätzlich geht man davon aus, dass
– die Note „ausreichend" das Erreichen von 45 % der Höchstpunktzahl voraussetzt,
– oberhalb der Note „ausreichend" die Zuordnung der Punktzahlen zu den Notenstufen linear verteilt ist: ab 59 % erlangst du die Note 3, ab 73 % Note 2 und ab 87 % Note 1,

- die Grenze zwischen den Noten „mangelhaft" und „ungenügend" bei etwa 18 % der Höchstpunktzahl liegt.

Mündliche Prüfung

Die mündliche Prüfung wird nicht zentral vom Schulministerium gestellt: Dein Englischlehrer oder deine Englischlehrerin formuliert die mündlichen Prüfungsaufgaben selbst. Geprüft wird der Stoff der Klasse 10, allerdings so, dass sich keine Überschneidungen zur schriftlichen Prüfung ergeben. Die Fachlehrerin/der Fachlehrer benennt drei Unterrichtsvorhaben aus der Jahrgangsstufe 10 als inhaltliche Grundlage. Die Aufgabenstellungen werden dir schriftlich vorgelegt. In einer 10-minütigen Vorbereitungszeit kannst du dich mit der Aufgabenstellung auseinandersetzen. Das Prüfungsgespräch dauert 15 Minuten. In der Regel beginnt die Prüfung mit einer kurzen, etwa dreiminütigen Einstimmung, in der dein Fachlehrer allgemeine Fragen stellt, damit du dich „aufwärmen" kannst. Im nächsten Prüfungsteil musst du dich zu bestimmten Sachverhalten äußern. Meist wird dir vor der Prüfung als Anhaltspunkt eine *mind map* oder ein kurzer Text mit Fragen vorgelegt. Nach diesem monologischen Teil sollst du zeigen, dass du auch in Gesprächen deine Meinung auf Englisch ausdrücken kannst. In diesem Teil tauschst du dich also mit den Prüfern zu einem bestimmten Thema aus. Dein Englischlehrer kann Zwischenfragen stellen, wenn er etwas genauer von dir wissen möchte oder wenn dir zu einem Thema nicht so viel einfällt.

Die Zeugnisnote setzt sich im Fall einer mündlichen Prüfung aus drei Noten zusammen:
- Vornote
- Note für die schriftliche Prüfungsleistung
- Note für die mündliche Prüfungsleistung

Diese Noten werden gewichtet im Verhältnis:
5 (Vornote) : 3 (schriftliche Prüfung) : 2 (mündliche Prüfung)

Eine weitere Nachprüfung ist in den Prüfungsfächern **nicht möglich**. Das bedeutet, dass du dich in den Fächern, in denen du eine Abschlussprüfung gemacht hast, nicht zu einer weiteren mündlichen Prüfung anmelden kannst, um zum Beispiel noch die Qualifikation für die Sekundarstufe II zu erreichen. Dies geht nur in den anderen Fächern.

Kurzgrammatik

Kurzgrammatik

Besonderheiten einiger Wortarten

1   Adjektive und Adverbien – *Adjectives and Adverbs*
Bildung und Verwendung von Adverbien – *Formation and Use of Adverbs*

Bildung

Adjektiv + *-ly*	glad	→ gladl<u>y</u>

Ausnahmen:

• *-y* am Wortende wird zu *-i*	eas<u>y</u>	→ eas<u>i</u>ly
	funn<u>y</u>	→ funn<u>i</u>ly
• auf einen Konsonanten folgendes *-le* wird zu *-ly*	simp<u>le</u>	→ simp<u>ly</u>
	probab<u>le</u>	→ probabl<u>y</u>
• *-ic* am Wortende wird zu *-ically*	fantast<u>ic</u>	→ fantast<u>ically</u>
Ausnahme:	pub<u>lic</u>	→ publicl<u>y</u>

Beachte:

• Unregelmäßig gebildet wird:	good	→ well

• Endet das Adjektiv auf *-ly*, so kann kein Adverb gebildet werden; man verwendet deshalb:
in a + Adjektiv + *manner/way* — friendly → in a friendly manner

• In einigen Fällen haben Adjektiv und Adverb dieselbe Form, z. B.: — daily, early, fast, hard, long, low, weekly, yearly

• Manche Adjektive bilden zwei Adverbformen, die sich in der Bedeutung unterscheiden, z. B.:

Adj./Adv.	Adv. auf *-ly*
hard	*hardly*
schwierig, hart	kaum
late	*lately*
spät	neulich, kürzlich
near	*nearly*
nahe	beinahe

The task is <u>hard</u>.   (adjective)
Die Aufgabe ist schwierig.
She works <u>hard</u>.   (adverb)
Sie arbeitet hart.
She <u>hardly</u> works.   (adverb)
Sie arbeitet kaum.

Verwendung

Adverbien bestimmen
- Verben,

She <u>easily</u> <u>found</u> her brother in the crowd.
Sie fand ihren Bruder leicht in der Menge.

- Adjektive,

This band is <u>extremely</u> <u>famous</u>.
Diese Band ist sehr berühmt.

- andere Adverbien oder

He walks <u>extremely</u> <u>quickly</u>.
Er geht äußerst schnell.

- einen ganzen Satz
näher.

<u>Fortunately</u>, <u>nobody was hurt</u>.
Glücklicherweise wurde niemand verletzt.

Beachte:

Nach bestimmten Verben steht nicht das Adverb, sondern das Adjektiv:
- Verben, die einen **Zustand** ausdrücken, z. B.:

to be	sein
to become	werden
to get	werden
to seem	scheinen
to stay	bleiben

Everything <u>seems</u> <u>quiet</u>.
Alles scheint ruhig zu sein.

- Verben der **Sinneswahrnehmung**, z. B.:

to feel	sich anfühlen
to look	aussehen
to smell	riechen
to sound	sich anhören
to taste	schmecken

This dress <u>looks</u> <u>fantastic</u>!
Dieses Kleid sieht toll aus!

Steigerung des Adjektivs – *Comparison of Adjectives*

Bildung

Man unterscheidet:
- Grundform / Positiv (*positive*)

Peter is <u>young</u>.

- Komparativ (*comparative*)

Jane is <u>younger</u>.

- Superlativ (*superlative*)

Paul is <u>the youngest</u>.

Steigerung auf -er, -est
- einsilbige Adjektive

old, old<u>er</u>, old<u>est</u>
alt, älter, am ältesten

- zweisilbige Adjektive, die auf -er, -le, -ow oder -y enden

clever, clever<u>er</u>, clever<u>est</u>
klug, klüger, am klügsten

simple, simpl<u>er</u>, simpl<u>est</u>
einfach, einfacher, am einfachsten

narrow, narrow<u>er</u>, narrow<u>est</u>
eng, enger, am engsten

funny, funn<u>ier</u>, funn<u>iest</u>
lustig, lustiger, am lustigsten

Beachte:
- stummes -e am Wortende entfällt

simpl<u>e</u>, simpl<u>er</u>, simpl<u>est</u>

- nach einem Konsonanten wird -y am Wortende zu -i-

funn<u>y</u>, funn<u>ier</u>, funn<u>iest</u>

- nach kurzem Vokal wird ein Konsonant am Wortende verdoppelt

fi<u>t</u>, fi<u>tter</u>, fi<u>ttest</u>

Steigerung mit more ..., most ...
- zweisilbige Adjektive, die nicht auf -er, -le, -ow oder -y enden

useful, <u>more</u> useful, <u>most</u> useful
nützlich, nützlicher, am nützlichsten

- Adjektive mit drei und mehr Silben

difficult, <u>more</u> difficult, <u>most</u> difficult
schwierig, schwieriger, am schwierigsten

Unregelmäßige Steigerung
Die unregelmäßig gesteigerten Adjektive muss man auswendig lernen. Einige sind hier angegeben:

good, better, best
gut, besser, am besten

bad, worse, worst
schlecht, schlechter, am schlechtesten

many, more, most
viele, mehr, am meisten

much, more, most
viel, mehr, am meisten

little, less, least
wenig, weniger, am wenigsten

Steigerungsformen im Satz – *Sentences with Comparisons*

Es gibt folgende Möglichkeiten,
Steigerungen im Satz zu verwenden:
- **Positiv:** Zwei oder mehr Personen oder Sachen sind **gleich oder ungleich:** *(not) as* + Grundform des Adjektivs + *as*

  Anne is <u>as</u> tall <u>as</u> John (and Steve).
  Anne ist genauso groß wie John (und Steve).

  John is <u>not as</u> tall <u>as</u> Steve.
  John ist nicht so groß wie Steve.

- **Komparativ:** Zwei oder mehr Personen/Sachen sind **verschieden** (größer/besser ...): Komparativform des Adjektivs + *than*

  Steve is <u>taller</u> <u>than</u> Anne.
  Steve ist größer als Anne.

- **Superlativ:** Eine Person oder Sache wird besonders hervorgehoben (der/die/das größte/ beste ...): *the* + Superlativform des Adjektivs

  Steve is <u>the tallest</u> boy in class.
  Steve ist der größte Junge in der Klasse.

Steigerung des Adverbs – *Comparison of Adverbs*

Adverbien können wie Adjektive auch gesteigert werden.
- Adverbien auf *-ly* werden mit *more, most* bzw. mit *less, least* gesteigert.

  She talks <u>more quickly</u> than John.
  Sie spricht schneller als John.

- Adverbien, die dieselbe Form wie das Adjektiv haben, werden mit *-er, -est* gesteigert.

fast –	fast<u>er</u> –	fast<u>est</u>
early –	earli<u>er</u> –	earli<u>est</u>

- Manche Adverbien haben unregelmäßige Steigerungsformen, z. B.:

well –	better –	best
badly –	worse –	worst
little –	less –	least
much –	more –	most

Die Stellung von Adverbien im Satz

Adverbien können verschiedene Positionen im Satz einnehmen:
- Am **Anfang des Satzes**, vor dem Subjekt *(front position)*

  <u>Tomorrow</u> he will be in London.
  Morgen [betont] wird er in London sein.
  <u>Unfortunately</u>, I can't come to the party.
  Leider kann ich nicht zur Party kommen.

- **Im Satz** *(mid position)*
  vor dem Vollverb,

  nach *to be,*

  nach dem ersten Hilfsverb.

- Am **Ende des Satzes** *(end position)*

Gibt es mehrere Adverbien am Satzende, so gilt die **Reihenfolge**: Art und Weise – Ort – Zeit *(manner – place – time)*

She <u>often</u> goes to school by bike.
Sie fährt oft mit dem Rad in die Schule.
She is <u>already</u> at home.
Sie ist schon zu Hause.
You can <u>even</u> go swimming there.
Man kann dort sogar schwimmen gehen.
He will be in London <u>tomorrow</u>.
Er wird morgen in London sein.

The snow melts <u>slowly</u> <u>in the mountains</u> <u>at springtime</u>.
Im Frühling schmilzt der Schnee langsam in den Bergen.

2 Artikel – *Article*

Der **bestimmte Artikel** steht, wenn man von einer **ganz bestimmten Person oder Sache** spricht.

Beachte: Der bestimmte Artikel steht unter anderem **immer** in folgenden Fällen:
- **abstrakte Begriffe**, die näher erläutert sind

- **Gebäudebezeichnungen**, wenn man vom Gebäude und nicht von der Institution spricht
- **Eigennamen im Plural** (Familien- namen, Gebirge, Inselgruppen, einige Länder etc.)
- Namen von **Flüssen** und **Meeren**

<u>The</u> cat is sleeping on the sofa.
Die Katze schläft auf dem Sofa. [nicht irgendeine Katze, sondern eine bestimmte]

<u>The</u> agriculture practised in the USA is very successful.
Die Landwirtschaft, wie sie in den USA praktiziert wird, ist sehr erfolgreich.
<u>The</u> university should be renovated soon.
Die Universität sollte bald renoviert werden.
<u>the</u> Johnsons, <u>the</u> Rockies, <u>the</u> Hebrides, <u>the</u> Netherlands, <u>the</u> USA

<u>the</u> Mississippi, <u>the</u> North Sea, <u>the</u> Pacific Ocean

Der **unbestimmte Artikel** steht, wenn man von einer **nicht näher bestimmten Person oder Sache** spricht.

<u>A</u> man is walking down the road.
Ein Mann läuft gerade die Straße entlang. [irgendein Mann]

Beachte:
In einigen Fällen steht **stets** der
unbestimmte Artikel:

- **Berufsbezeichnungen** und
  Nationalitäten

  She is <u>an</u> engineer. *Sie ist Ingenieurin.*
  He is <u>a</u> Scot(sman). *Er ist Schotte.*

- Zugehörigkeit zu einer **Religion**
  oder **Partei**

  She is <u>a</u> Catholic. *Sie ist katholisch.*
  He is <u>a</u> Tory. *Er ist Mitglied der Tories.*

In diesen Fällen steht **kein Artikel:**

- **nicht zählbare** Nomen wie z. B.
  Stoffbezeichnungen

  Gold is very valuable.
  Gold ist sehr wertvoll.

- **abstrakte Nomen** ohne nähere
  Bestimmung

  Buddhism is widespread in Asia.
  Der Buddhismus ist in Asien weit verbreitet.

- **Kollektivbegriffe**, z. B. *man,*
  youth, society

  Man is responsible for global warming.
  Der Mensch ist für die Klimaerwärmung
  verantwortlich.

- **Institutionen**, z. B. *school, church,*
  university, prison

  We went to school together.
  Wir gingen zusammen zur Schule.

- **Mahlzeiten**, z. B. *breakfast, lunch*

  Dinner is at 8 p.m.
  Das Abendessen ist um 20 Uhr.

- *by* + **Verkehrsmittel**

  I went to school by bike.
  Ich fuhr mit dem Fahrrad zur Schule.

- **Personennamen** (auch mit Titel),
  Verwandtschaftsbezeichnungen,
  die wie Namen verwendet werden

  Tom, Mr Scott, Queen Elizabeth, Dr Hill,
  Dad, Uncle Harry

- Bezeichnungen für **Straßen,**
  Plätze, Brücken, Parkanlagen

  Fifth Avenue, Trafalgar Square, Westminster Bridge, Hyde Park

- Namen von **Ländern, Kontinen-**
  ten, Städten, Seen, Inseln, Bergen

  France, Asia, San Francisco, Loch Ness,
  Corsica, Ben Nevis

3 Pronomen – *Pronouns*

Possessivpronomen – *Possessive Pronouns*

Possessivpronomen *(possessive*
pronouns) verwendet man, um zu
sagen, **wem etwas gehört.**
Steht ein Possessivpronomen allein,
so wird eine andere Form verwendet
als in Verbindung mit einem Substantiv:

mit Substantiv	ohne Substantiv
my	*mine*
your	*yours*
his/her/its	*his/hers/–*
our	*ours*
your	*yours*
their	*theirs*

This is <u>my bike</u>.   –   This is <u>mine</u>.

This is <u>your bike</u>.   –   This is <u>yours</u>.

This is <u>her bike</u>.   –   This is <u>hers</u>.

This is <u>our bike</u>.   –   This is <u>ours</u>.

This is <u>your bike</u>.   –   This is <u>yours</u>.

This is <u>their bike</u>.   –   This is <u>theirs</u>.

Reflexivpronomen – *Reflexive Pronouns*

Reflexivpronomen *(reflexive pronouns)* **beziehen sich auf das Subjekt** des Satzes **zurück**. Es handelt sich also um dieselbe Person:

myself

yourself

himself / herself / itself

ourselves

yourselves

themselves

<u>I</u> will buy <u>myself</u> a new car.

<u>You</u> will buy <u>yourself</u> a new car.

<u>He</u> will buy <u>himself</u> a new car.

<u>We</u> will buy <u>ourselves</u> a new car.

<u>You</u> will buy <u>yourselves</u> a new car.

<u>They</u> will buy <u>themselves</u> a new car.

Beachte:

- Einige Verben stehen ohne Reflexivpronomen, obwohl im Deutschen mit „mich, dich, sich etc." übersetzt wird.

I apologize …
Ich entschuldige <u>mich</u> …
He is hiding.
Er versteckt <u>sich</u>.

- Einige Verben können sowohl mit einem Objekt als auch mit einem Reflexivpronomen verwendet werden. Dabei ändert sich die Bedeutung, z. B. bei *to control, to enjoy, to help, to occupy.*

He is enjoying <u>the party</u>.
Er genießt die Party.
She is enjoying <u>herself</u>.
Sie amüsiert sich.

He is helping <u>the child</u>.
Er hilft dem Kind.
Help y<u>ourself</u>!
Bedienen Sie sich!

Reziprokes Pronomen – *Reciprocal Pronoun* ("each other/one another")

each other/one another ist unveränderlich. Es bezieht sich auf **zwei oder mehr Personen** und wird mit „sich (gegenseitig)/einander" übersetzt.	They looked at <u>each other</u> and laughed. *Sie schauten sich (gegenseitig) an und lachten.* *oder:* *Sie schauten einander an und lachten.*
Beachte: Einige Verben stehen ohne *each other*, obwohl im Deutschen mit „sich" übersetzt wird.	to meet *sich treffen* to kiss *sich küssen* to fall in love *sich verlieben*

4 Präpositionen – *Prepositions*

Präpositionen *(prepositions)* drücken **räumliche, zeitliche oder andere Arten von Beziehungen** aus.

The ball is <u>under</u> the table.
He came home <u>after</u> six o'clock.

Die wichtigsten Präpositionen mit Beispielen für ihre Verwendung:
- *at*
  Ortsangabe: *at home*

  I'm <u>at home</u> now. *Ich bin jetzt zu Hause.*

  Zeitangabe: *at 3 p.m.*

  He arrived <u>at 3 p.m.</u> *Er kam um 15 Uhr an.*

- *by*
  Angabe des Mittels: *by bike*

  She went to work <u>by bike</u>. *Sie fuhr mit dem Rad zur Arbeit.*

  Angabe der Ursache: *by mistake*

  He did it <u>by mistake</u>. *Er hat es aus Versehen getan.*

  Zeitangabe: *by tomorrow*

  You will get the letter <u>by tomorrow</u>. *Du bekommst den Brief bis morgen.*

- *for*
  Zeitdauer: *for hours*

  We waited for the bus <u>for hours</u>. *Wir warteten stundenlang auf den Bus.*

- *from*
  Ortsangabe: *from Dublin*

  Ian is <u>from Dublin</u>. *Ian kommt aus Dublin.*

  Zeitangabe: *from nine to five*

  We work <u>from nine to five</u>. *Wir arbeiten von neun bis fünf Uhr.*

- *in*
  Ortsangabe: *in England*

  <u>In England</u>, they drive on the left. *In England herrscht Linksverkehr.*

Zeitangabe: *in the morning*	They woke up <u>in the morning</u>. *Sie wachten am Morgen auf.*
• *of* Ortsangabe: *north of the city*	The village lies <u>north of the city</u>. *Das Dorf liegt nördlich der Stadt.*
• *on* Ortsangabe: *on the left,* *on the floor*	<u>On the left</u> you see the London Eye. *Links sehen Sie das London Eye.*
Zeitangabe: *on Monday*	<u>On Monday</u> she will buy the tickets. *(Am) Montag kauft sie die Karten.*
• *to* Richtungsangabe: *to the left*	Please turn <u>to the left</u>. *Bitte wenden Sie sich nach links.*
Angabe des Ziels: *to London*	He goes <u>to London</u> every year. *Er fährt jedes Jahr nach London.*

5 Modale Hilfsverben – *Modal Auxiliaries*

Zu den **modalen Hilfsverben** *(modal auxiliaries)* zählen z. B. *can, may* und *must*.

Bildung

- Die modalen Hilfsverben haben für alle Personen **nur eine Form**: kein *-s* in der 3. Person Singular.

I, you, he/she/it,
we, you, they $\Big\}$ must

- Auf ein modales Hilfsverb folgt der **Infinitiv ohne** *to*.

You <u>must</u> listen to my new CD.
Du musst dir meine neue CD anhören.

- **Frage und Verneinung** werden nicht mit *do/did* umschrieben.

<u>Can</u> you help me, please?
Kannst du mir bitte helfen?

Die modalen Hilfsverben können nicht alle Zeiten bilden. Deshalb benötigt man **Ersatzformen** (können auch im Präsens verwendet werden).

- *can* (können)
Ersatzformen:
(to) be able to (Fähigkeit),
(to) be allowed to (Erlaubnis)

I <u>can</u> sing./I <u>was able to</u> sing.
Ich kann singen. / Ich konnte singen.

You <u>can't</u> go to the party./
I <u>wasn't allowed to</u> go to the party.
Du darfst nicht auf die Party gehen./
Ich durfte nicht auf die Party gehen.

Beachte: Im *simple past* und *conditional I* ist auch *could* möglich.

When I was three, I <u>could</u> already ski.
Mit drei konnte ich schon Ski fahren.

- *may* (dürfen) – sehr höflich
  Ersatzform: *(to) be allowed to*

  You <u>may</u> go home early. /
  You <u>were allowed to</u> go home early.
  Du darfst früh nach Hause gehen. /
  Du durftest früh nach Hause gehen.

- *must* (müssen)
  Ersatzform: *(to) have to*

  He <u>must</u> be home by ten o'clock. /
  He <u>had to</u> be home by ten o'clock.
  Er muss um zehn Uhr zu Hause sein. /
  Er musste um zehn Uhr zu Hause sein.

Beachte:
must not/mustn't = „nicht dürfen"

You <u>must not</u> eat all the cake.
Du darfst nicht den ganzen Kuchen essen.

„nicht müssen, nicht brauchen" =
not have to, needn't

You <u>don't have to</u> / <u>needn't</u> eat all the cake.
Du musst nicht den ganzen Kuchen essen. /
Du brauchst nicht ... zu essen.

Infinitiv, Gerundium oder Partizip? – Die infiniten Verbformen

6 Infinitiv – *Infinitive*

Der **Infinitiv** (Grundform des Verbs)
mit *to* steht z. B. **nach**
- bestimmten **Verben**, z. B.:

to decide	(sich) entscheiden, beschließen
to expect	erwarten
to hope	hoffen
to manage	schaffen
to plan	planen
to promise	versprechen
to want	wollen

He <u>decided to wait</u>.
Er beschloss zu warten.

- bestimmten **Substantiven und Pronomen** *(something, anything)*, z. B.:

attempt	Versuch
idea	Idee
plan	Plan
wish	Wunsch

We haven't got <u>anything</u> <u>to eat</u> at home.
Wir haben nichts zu essen zu Hause.

It was her <u>plan</u> <u>to visit</u> him in May.
Sie hatte vor, ihn im Mai zu besuchen.

- bestimmten **Adjektiven** (auch in Verbindung mit *too / enough*) und deren Steigerungsformen, z. B.:

certain	sicher
difficult / hard	schwer, schwierig
easy	leicht

It was <u>difficult</u> <u>to follow</u> her.
Es war schwer, ihr zu folgen.

- **Fragewörtern**, wie z. B. *what, where, which, who, when, how* und nach *whether*. Diese Konstruktion ersetzt eine indirekte Frage mit modalem Hilfsverb.

We knew <u>where</u> to find her. /
We knew <u>where</u> <u>we</u> would find her.
Wir wussten, wo wir sie finden würden.

Die Konstruktion **Objekt + Infinitiv** wird im Deutschen oft mit einem „dass"-Satz übersetzt.
Sie steht z. B. **nach**

- bestimmten **Verben**, z. B.:

to allow	erlauben
to get	veranlassen
to help	helfen
to persuade	überreden

She <u>allowed</u> <u>him</u> <u>to go</u> to the cinema.
Sie erlaubte ihm, dass er ins Kino geht. / … ins Kino zu gehen.

- **Verb + Präposition**, z. B.:

to count on	rechnen mit
to rely on	sich verlassen auf
to wait for	warten auf

She <u>relies on</u> <u>him</u> <u>to arrive</u> in time.
Sie verlässt sich darauf, dass er rechtzeitig ankommt.

- **Adjektiv + Präposition**, z. B.:

easy for	leicht
necessary for	notwendig
nice of	nett
silly of	dumm

It is <u>necessary</u> <u>for you</u> <u>to learn</u> maths.
Es ist notwendig, dass du Mathe lernst.

- **Substantiv + Präposition**, z. B.:

opportunity for	Gelegenheit
idea for	Idee
time for	Zeit
mistake for	Fehler

Work experience is a good <u>opportunity</u> <u>for you</u> <u>to find out</u> which job suits you.
Ein Praktikum ist eine gute Gelegenheit, herauszufinden, welcher Beruf zu dir passt.

- einem **Adjektiv**, das durch *too* oder *enough* näher bestimmt wird.

The box is <u>too</u> heavy <u>for me</u> <u>to carry</u>.
Die Kiste ist mir zu schwer zum Tragen.

The weather is <u>good</u> <u>enough</u> <u>for us</u> <u>to go</u> for a walk. *Das Wetter ist gut genug, dass wir spazieren gehen können.*

7 Gerundium (-*ing*-Form) – *Gerund*

Bildung
Infinitiv + *-ing*

read → read<u>ing</u>

Beachte:

- stummes *-e* entfällt   wri<u>te</u> → writ<u>ing</u>
- nach kurzem betontem Vokal: sto<u>p</u> → sto<u>pp</u>ing
  Schlusskonsonant verdoppelt
- *-ie* wird zu *-y*   l<u>ie</u> → l<u>y</u>ing

Verwendung
Die *-ing*-Form steht nach bestimmten
Ausdrücken und kann verschiedene
Funktionen im Satz einnehmen, z. B.:

- als **Subjekt** des Satzes   <u>Skiing</u> is fun. *Skifahren macht Spaß.*

- nach bestimmten **Verben**
  (als **Objekt** des Satzes), z. B.:

to avoid	vermeiden
to enjoy	genießen, gern tun
to keep (on)	weitermachen
to miss	vermissen
to risk	riskieren
to suggest	vorschlagen

He <u>enjoys</u> <u>reading</u> comics.
Er liest gerne Comics.

You <u>risk</u> <u>losing</u> a friend.
Du riskierst, einen Freund zu verlieren.

- nach **Verb + Präposition**, z. B.:

to agree with	zustimmen
to believe in	glauben an
to dream of	träumen von
to look forward to	sich freuen auf
to talk about	sprechen über

She <u>dreams</u> <u>of</u> <u>meeting</u> a star.
Sie träumt davon, einen Star zu treffen.

- nach **Adjektiv + Präposition**, z. B.:

afraid of	sich fürchten vor
famous for	berühmt für
good/bad at	gut/schlecht in
interested in	interessiert an

He is <u>afraid</u> <u>of</u> <u>losing</u> his job.
Er hat Angst, seine Arbeit zu verlieren.

- nach **Substantiv + Präposition**,
  z B.:

chance of	Chance, Aussicht
danger of	Gefahr
reason for	Grund
way of	Art und Weise

Do you have a <u>chance</u> <u>of</u> <u>getting</u> the job?
Hast du Aussicht, die Stelle zu bekommen?

- nach **Präpositionen** und **Konjunktionen der Zeit**, z. B.:

after	nachdem
before	bevor
by	indem,
	dadurch, dass
in spite of	trotz
instead of	statt

Before leaving the room he said goodbye.
Bevor er den Raum verließ, verabschiedete er sich.

8 Infinitiv oder Gerundium? – *Infinitive or Gerund?*

Einige Verben können sowohl **mit dem Infinitiv** als auch **mit der -ing-Form** stehen, **ohne** dass sich die **Bedeutung ändert**, z. B.
to love, to hate, to prefer, to start, to begin, to continue.

I hate getting up early.
I hate to get up early.
Ich hasse es, früh aufzustehen.

Bei manchen Verben **ändert sich** jedoch die **Bedeutung**, je nachdem, ob sie mit Infinitiv oder mit der -ing-Form verwendet werden, z. B.
to remember, to forget, to stop.

- *to remember* + Infinitiv:
  „daran denken, etwas zu tun"

  I must remember to post the invitations.
  Ich muss daran denken, die Einladungen einzuwerfen.

  to remember + ing-Form:
  „sich erinnern, etwas getan zu haben"

  I remember posting the invitations.
  Ich erinnere mich daran, die Einladungen eingeworfen zu haben.

- *to forget* + Infinitiv:
  „vergessen, etwas zu tun"

  Don't forget to water the plants.
  Vergiss nicht, die Pflanzen zu gießen.

  to forget + ing-Form:
  „vergessen, etwas getan zu haben"

  I'll never forget meeting the President.
  Ich werde nie vergessen, wie ich den Präsidenten traf.

- *to stop* + Infinitiv:
  „stehen bleiben, um etwas zu tun"

  I stopped to read the road sign.
  Ich hielt an, um das Verkehrsschild zu lesen.

  to stop + ing-Form:
  „aufhören, etwas zu tun"

  He stopped laughing.
  Er hörte auf zu lachen.

9 Partizipien – *Participles*

Partizip Präsens – *Present Participle*

Bildung
Infinitiv + *ing*
Sonderformen: siehe *gerund*
(S. G 11 f.)

talk → talking

Verwendung
Das *present participle* verwendet man:

- zur Bildung der Verlaufsform
  present progressive,

  Peter is <u>reading</u>.
  Peter liest (gerade).

- zur Bildung der Verlaufsform
  past progressive,

  Peter was <u>reading</u> when I saw him.
  Peter las (gerade), als ich ihn sah.

- zur Bildung der Verlaufsform
  present perfect progressive,

  I have been <u>living</u> in Sydney for 5 years.
  Ich lebe seit 5 Jahren in Sydney.

- zur Bildung der Verlaufsform
  future progressive,

  This time tomorrow I will be <u>working</u>.
  Morgen um diese Zeit werde ich arbeiten.

- wie ein Adjektiv, wenn es vor
  einem Substantiv steht.

  The village hasn't got <u>running</u> water.
  Das Dorf hat kein fließendes Wasser.

Partizip Perfekt – *Past Participle*

Bildung
Infinitiv + *-ed*

talk → talk<u>ed</u>

Beachte:

- stummes *-e* entfällt

  liv<u>e</u> → liv<u>ed</u>

- nach kurzem betontem Vokal wird
  der Schlusskonsonant verdoppelt

  sto<u>p</u> → stop<u>ped</u>

- *-y* wird zu *-ie*

- unregelmäßige Verben
  (S. G 31 f.)

  cr<u>y</u> → cr<u>ied</u>
  be → been

Verwendung
Das *past participle* verwendet man

- zur Bildung des *present perfect,*

  He hasn't <u>talked</u> to Tom yet.
  Er hat noch nicht mit Tom gesprochen.

- zur Bildung des *past perfect*,

Before they went biking in France, they had <u>bought</u> new bikes.
Bevor sie nach Frankreich zum Radfahren gingen, hatten sie neue Fahrräder gekauft.

- zur Bildung des *future perfect*,

The letter will have <u>arrived</u> by then.
Der Brief wird bis dann angekommen sein.

- zur Bildung des Passivs,

The fish was <u>eaten</u> by the cat.
Der Fisch wurde von der Katze gefressen.

- wie ein Adjektiv, wenn es vor einem Substantiv steht.

Peter has got a well-<u>paid</u> job.
Peter hat eine gut bezahlte Stelle.

Verkürzung eines Nebensatzes durch ein Partizip

Adverbiale Nebensätze (meist kausale oder temporale Bedeutung) und **Relativsätze** können durch ein Partizip verkürzt werden.

She watches the news, because she wants to stay informed.
<u>Wanting</u> to stay informed, she watches the news.
Sie sieht sich die Nachrichten an, weil sie informiert bleiben möchte.

Aus der Zeitform des Verbs im Nebensatz ergibt sich, welches Partizip für die Satzverkürzung verwendet wird:

- Steht das Verb im Nebensatz im *present* oder *past tense* (*simple* und *progressive form*), verwendet man das *present participle*.

$$\left.\begin{array}{l}\text{he finishes}\\\text{he finished}\end{array}\right\} \rightarrow \text{finishing}$$

- Steht das Verb im Nebensatz im *present perfect* oder *past perfect*, verwendet man *having* + *past participle*.

$$\left.\begin{array}{l}\text{he has finished}\\\text{he had finished}\end{array}\right\} \rightarrow \text{having finished}$$

- Das *past participle* verwendet man auch, um einen Satz im Passiv zu verkürzen.

Sally is a manager in a five-star hotel <u>which is called</u> Pacific View.
Sally is a manager in a five-star hotel <u>called</u> Pacific View.

Beachte:
- Man kann einen Temporal- oder Kausalsatz verkürzen, wenn **Haupt- und Nebensatz dasselbe Subjekt** haben.

When <u>he</u> was walking down the street, <u>he</u> saw Jo.
(When) <u>walking</u> down the street, <u>he</u> saw Jo.
Als er die Straße entlangging, sah er Jo.

G 15

- Bei **Kausalsätzen** entfallen die Konjunktionen *as, because* und *since* im verkürzten Nebensatz.

As <u>he</u> was hungry, <u>he</u> bought a sandwich.
<u>Being</u> hungry, <u>he</u> bought a sandwich.
Da er hungrig war, kaufte er ein Sandwich.

- In einem **Temporalsatz** bleibt die einleitende **Konjunktion** häufig erhalten, um dem Satz eine **eindeutige Bedeutung** zuzuweisen.

When <u>he</u> left, <u>he</u> forgot to lock the door.
<u>When</u> <u>leaving</u>, <u>he</u> forgot to lock the door.
Als er ging, vergaß er, die Tür abzuschließen.

Tara got sick <u>eating</u> too much chocolate.
Tara wurde schlecht, als/während/da sie zu viel Schokolade aß.

Die Vorzeitigkeit einer Handlung kann durch *after + present participle* oder durch *having + past participle* ausgedrückt werden.

<u>After</u> <u>finishing</u> / <u>Having finished</u> breakfast, he went to work.
Nachdem er sein Frühstück beendet hatte, ging er zur Arbeit.

- Bei **Relativsätzen** entfallen die Relativpronomen *who, which* und *that*.

I saw a six-year-old boy <u>who</u> <u>played</u> the piano.
I saw a six-year-old boy <u>playing</u> the piano.
Ich sah einen sechsjährigen Jungen, der gerade Klavier spielte. / ... Klavier spielen.

Verbindung von zwei Hauptsätzen durch ein Partizip

Zwei Hauptsätze können durch ein Partizip verbunden werden, wenn sie **dasselbe Subjekt** haben.

Beachte:

- Das Subjekt des zweiten Hauptsatzes und die Konjunktion *and* entfallen.
- Die Verbform des zweiten Hauptsatzes wird durch das Partizip ersetzt.

<u>He</u> did his homework and <u>he</u> listened to the radio.
<u>He</u> did his homework <u>listening</u> to the radio.
Er machte seine Hausaufgaben und hörte Radio.

Unverbundene Partizipialkonstruktionen haben ein **eigenes Subjekt**, das nicht mit dem Subjekt des Hauptsatzes übereinstimmt. Sie werden in **gehobener Sprache** verwendet.
Mit einleitendem ***with*** werden sie auf allen Stilebenen verwendet.

The <u>sun</u> having come out, the ladies went for a walk in the park.
Da die Sonne herausgekommen war, gingen die Damen im Park spazieren.

With the <u>telephone</u> ringing, she jumped out of bed.
Als das Telefon klingelte, sprang sie aus dem Bett.

Bildung und Gebrauch der finiten Verbformen

10 Zeiten – *Tenses*

Simple Present

Bildung
Infinitiv, Ausnahme 3. Person Singular: Infinitiv + *-s*

stand – he/she/it stand<u>s</u>

Beachte:
- Bei Verben, die auf *-s, -sh, -ch, -x* und *-z* enden, wird in der 3. Person Singular *-es* angefügt.

kiss – he/she/it kiss<u>es</u>
rush – he/she/it rush<u>es</u>
teach – he/she/it teach<u>es</u>
fix – he/she/it fix<u>es</u>

- Bei Verben, die auf Konsonant + *-y* enden, wird *-es* angefügt; *-y* wird zu *-i-*.

carry – he/she/it carr<u>ies</u>

Bildung von Fragen im *simple present*
(Fragewort +) *do/does* + Subjekt + Infinitiv

<u>Where</u> <u>does</u> <u>he</u> <u>live</u>? / <u>Does</u> <u>he</u> <u>live</u> in London?
Wo lebt er? / Lebt er in London?

Beachte:
Die Umschreibung mit *do/does* wird nicht verwendet,
- wenn nach dem Subjekt gefragt wird (mit *who, what, which*),

<u>Who</u> likes pizza?
Wer mag Pizza?

<u>Which</u> tree <u>has</u> more leaves?
Welcher Baum hat mehr Blätter?

- wenn die Frage mit *is/are* gebildet wird.

<u>Are</u> you happy?
Bist du glücklich?

Bildung der Verneinung im *simple present*
don't/doesn't + Infinitiv

He <u>doesn't like</u> football.
Er mag Fußball nicht.

Verwendung
Das *simple present* wird verwendet:
- bei Tätigkeiten, die man **gewohnheitsmäßig** oder häufig ausführt
Signalwörter: z. B. *always, often, never, every day, every morning, every afternoon*

Every morning John <u>buys</u> a newspaper.
Jeden Morgen kauft John eine Zeitung.

- bei **allgemeingültigen** Aussagen

London <u>is</u> a big city.
London ist eine große Stadt.

- bei **Zustandsverben**: Sie drücken Eigenschaften / Zustände von Personen und Dingen aus und stehen normalerweise nur in der *simple form*, z. B. *to hate, to know, to like.*

I like science-fiction films.
Ich mag Science-Fiction-Filme.

Present Progressive / Present Continuous

Bildung
am/is/are + *present participle*

read → <u>am/is/are</u> <u>reading</u>

Bildung von Fragen im *present progressive*
(Fragewort +) *am/is/are* + Subjekt + *present participle*

<u>Is</u> Peter <u>reading</u>? / What <u>is</u> he <u>reading</u>?
Liest Peter gerade? / Was liest er?

Bildung der Verneinung im *present progressive*
am not/isn't/aren't + *present participle*

Peter <u>isn't</u> <u>reading</u>.
Peter liest gerade nicht.

Verwendung
Mit dem *present progressive* drückt man aus, dass etwas **gerade passiert** und **noch nicht abgeschlossen** ist. Es wird daher auch als **Verlaufsform** der Gegenwart bezeichnet.

Signalwörter: *at the moment, now*

At the moment, Peter <u>is drinking</u> a cup of tea.
Im Augenblick trinkt Peter eine Tasse Tee.
[Er hat damit angefangen und noch nicht aufgehört.]

Simple Past

Bildung
Regelmäßige Verben: Infinitiv + *-ed*

walk → walk**ed**

Beachte:
- stummes *-e* entfällt

hope → hop**ed**

- Bei Verben, die auf Konsonant +
  -y enden, wird *-y* zu *-i-*.

carry → carr**ied**

- Nach kurzem betontem Vokal
  wird der Schlusskonsonant verdoppelt.

stop → sto**pped**

Unregelmäßige Verben: siehe Liste
S. G 31 f.

be → was

have → had

Bildung von Fragen im *simple past*
(Fragewort +) *did* + Subjekt +
Infinitiv

<u>(Why)</u> <u>Did</u> <u>he</u> <u>look</u> out of the window?
(Warum) Sah er aus dem Fenster?

Beachte:
Die Umschreibung mit *did* wird nicht
verwendet,
- wenn nach dem Subjekt gefragt
  wird (mit *who, what, which*),

<u>Who</u> <u>paid</u> the bill?
Wer zahlte die Rechnung?

<u>What</u> <u>happened</u> to your friend?
Was ist mit deinem Freund passiert?

- wenn die Frage mit *was/were*
  gebildet wird.

<u>Were</u> you happy?
Warst du glücklich?

Bildung der Verneinung im *simple*
past
didn't + Infinitiv

He <u>didn't</u> <u>call</u> me.
Er rief mich nicht an.

Verwendung
Das *simple past* beschreibt Handlungen und Ereignisse, die **in der**
Vergangenheit passierten und
bereits abgeschlossen sind.

Signalwörter: z. B. *yesterday, last*
week/year, two years ago, in 2008

Last week, he <u>helped</u> me with my homework.
Letzte Woche half er mir bei meinen Haus-
aufgaben. [Die Handlung fand in der letzten
Woche statt, ist also abgeschlossen.]

Past Progressive / Past Continuous

Bildung
was/were + present participle

watch → <u>was/were</u> <u>watching</u>

Verwendung
Die **Verlaufsform** *past progressive* verwendet man, wenn **zu einem bestimmten Zeitpunkt** in der Vergangenheit eine **Handlung ablief**, bzw. wenn eine **Handlung** von einer anderen **unterbrochen** wurde.

Yesterday at 9 o'clock I <u>was</u> still <u>sleeping</u>.
Gestern um 9 Uhr schlief ich noch.

I <u>was reading</u> a book when Peter came into the room.
Ich las (gerade) ein Buch, als Peter ins Zimmer kam.

Present Perfect (Simple)

Bildung
have/has + past participle

write → <u>has/have</u> <u>written</u>

Verwendung
Das *present perfect* verwendet man,
- wenn ein Vorgang **in der Vergangenheit begonnen** hat und **noch andauert**,

- wenn das Ergebnis einer vergangenen Handlung **Auswirkungen auf die Gegenwart** hat.

He <u>has lived</u> in London since 2008.
Er lebt seit 2008 in London.
[Er lebt jetzt immer noch in London.]

I <u>have</u> just <u>cleaned</u> my car.
Ich habe gerade mein Auto geputzt.
[Man sieht evtl. das saubere Auto.]

Signalwörter: z. B. *already, ever, just, how long, not ... yet, since, for*

Have you <u>ever</u> been to Dublin?
Warst du schon jemals in Dublin?

Beachte:
- *have/has* können zu *'ve/'s* verkürzt werden.

- Das *present perfect* wird oft mit *since* und *for* verwendet („seit").
  – *since* gibt einen **Zeitpunkt** an:

  – *for* gibt einen **Zeitraum** an:

He<u>'s</u> given me his umbrella.
Er hat mir seinen Regenschirm gegeben.

Ron has lived in Sydney <u>since 2007</u>.
Ron lebt seit 2007 in Sydney.

Sally has lived in Berlin <u>for five years</u>.
Sally lebt seit fünf Jahren in Berlin.

Present Perfect Progressive / Present Perfect Continuous

Bildung
have/has + been + present participle

write ➝ has/have been writing

Verwendung
Die **Verlaufsform** *present perfect progressive* verwendet man, um die **Dauer einer Handlung** zu **betonen**, die in der Vergangenheit begonnen hat und noch andauert.

She has been sleeping for ten hours.
Sie schläft seit zehn Stunden.

Past Perfect (Simple)

Bildung
had + past participle

write ➝ had written

Verwendung
Die Vorvergangenheit *past perfect* verwendet man, wenn ein Vorgang in der Vergangenheit **vor einem anderen Vorgang in der Vergangenheit abgeschlossen** wurde.

He had bought a ticket before he took the train to Manchester.
Er hatte eine Fahrkarte gekauft, bevor er den Zug nach Manchester nahm. [Beim Einsteigen war der Kauf abgeschlossen.]

Past Perfect Progressive / Past Perfect Continuous

Bildung
had + been + present participle

write ➝ had been writing

Verwendung
Die **Verlaufsform** *past perfect progressive* verwendet man für **Handlungen**, die in der Vergangenheit **bis zu dem Zeitpunkt andauerten**, zu dem eine neue Handlung einsetzte.

She had been sleeping for ten hours when the doorbell rang.
Sie hatte seit zehn Stunden geschlafen, als es an der Tür klingelte. [Das Schlafen dauerte bis zu dem Zeitpunkt an, als es an der Tür klingelte.]

Will-future

Bildung
will + Infinitiv

buy → <u>will</u> <u>buy</u>

Bildung von Fragen im
will-future
(Fragewort +) *will* + Subjekt +
Infinitiv

<u>What</u> <u>will</u> <u>you</u> <u>buy</u>?
Was wirst du kaufen?

Bildung der Verneinung im
will-future
won't + Infinitiv

Why <u>won't</u> you <u>come</u> to our party?
Warum kommst du nicht zu unserer Party?

Verwendung
Das *will-future* verwendet man, wenn
ein Vorgang **in der Zukunft
stattfinden** wird:
* bei Vorhersagen oder Vermutun-
gen,

* bei spontanen Entscheidungen.

The weather <u>will</u> <u>be</u> fine tomorrow.
Das Wetter wird morgen schön (sein).

[doorbell] "<u>I'll</u> <u>open</u> the door."
"Ich werde die Tür öffnen."

Signalwörter: z. B. *tomorrow,
next week, next Monday, next year,
in three years, soon*

Going-to-future

Bildung
am/is/are + *going to* + Infinitiv

find → <u>am/is/are</u> <u>going to</u> <u>find</u>

Verwendung
Das *going-to-future* verwendet man,
wenn man ausdrücken will:
* was man für die Zukunft **plant**
oder **zu tun beabsichtigt.**

* dass ein **Ereignis bald eintreten
wird**, da bestimmte **Anzeichen**
vorhanden sind.

I <u>am going to work</u> in England this summer.
*Diesen Sommer werde ich in England
arbeiten.*

Look at those clouds. It's <u>going to rain</u> soon.
*Schau dir diese Wolken an. Es wird bald
regnen.*

Simple Present und Present Progressive zur Wiedergabe der Zukunft

Verwendung

- Mit dem *present progressive* drückt man **Pläne** für die Zukunft aus, für die bereits **Vorkehrungen** getroffen wurden.

We <u>are flying</u> to New York tomorrow.
Morgen fliegen wir nach New York.
[Wir haben schon Tickets.]

- Mit dem *simple present* wird ein zukünftiges Geschehen wiedergegeben, das **von außen festgelegt** wurde, z. B. Fahrpläne, Programme, Kalender.

The train <u>leaves</u> at 8.15 a.m.
Der Zug fährt um 8.15 Uhr.
The play <u>ends</u> at 10 p.m.
Das Theaterstück endet um 22 Uhr.

Future Progressive / Future Continuous

Bildung
will + be + present participle

work → <u>will</u> <u>be</u> <u>working</u>

Verwendung
Die **Verlaufsform** *future progressive* drückt aus, dass ein **Vorgang** in der Zukunft zu einem bestimmten Zeitpunkt **gerade ablaufen wird**.

This time tomorrow I <u>will</u> <u>be</u> <u>sitting</u> in a plane to London.
Morgen um diese Zeit werde ich gerade im Flugzeug nach London sitzen.

Signalwörter: *this time next week / tomorrow, tomorrow* + Zeitangabe

Future Perfect (Future II)

Bildung
will + have + past participle

go → <u>will</u> <u>have</u> <u>gone</u>

Verwendung
Das *future perfect* drückt aus, dass ein **Vorgang** in der Zukunft **abgeschlossen sein wird** (Vorzeitigkeit in der Zukunft).

By 5 p.m. tomorrow I <u>will</u> <u>have</u> <u>arrived</u> in London.
Morgen Nachmittag um fünf Uhr werde ich bereits in London angekommen sein.

Signalwörter: *by then, by* + Zeitangabe

11 Passiv – *Passive Voice*

Bildung

Form von *(to) be* in der entsprechenden Zeitform + *past participle*

The bridge <u>was</u> <u>finished</u> in 1894.
Die Brücke wurde 1894 fertiggestellt.

Zeitformen:

* *simple present*

  Aktiv: Joe <u>buys</u> the milk.
  Passiv: The milk <u>is bought</u> by Joe.

* *simple past*

  Aktiv: Joe <u>bought</u> the milk.
  Passiv: The milk <u>was bought</u> by Joe.

* *present perfect*

  Aktiv: Joe <u>has bought</u> the milk.
  Passiv: The milk <u>has been</u> bought by Joe.

* *past perfect*

  Aktiv: Joe <u>had bought</u> the milk.
  Passiv: The milk <u>had been</u> bought by Joe.

* *will-future*

  Aktiv: Joe <u>will buy</u> the milk.
  Passiv: The milk <u>will be</u> bought by Joe.

* *future perfect (future II)*

  Aktiv: Joe <u>will have bought</u> the milk.
  Passiv: The milk <u>will have been</u> bought by Joe.

* *conditional I*

  Aktiv: Joe <u>would buy</u> the milk.
  Passiv: The milk <u>would be</u> bought by Joe.

* *conditional II*

  Aktiv: Joe <u>would have bought</u> the milk.
  Passiv: The milk <u>would have been</u> bought by Joe.

Aktiv → Passiv

* Das Subjekt des Aktivsatzes wird zum Objekt des Passivsatzes. Es wird mit *by* angeschlossen.
* Das Objekt des Aktivsatzes wird zum Subjekt des Passivsatzes.
* Stehen im Aktiv **zwei Objekte**, lassen sich zwei verschiedene Passivsätze bilden. Ein Objekt wird zum Subjekt des Passivsatzes, das zweite bleibt Objekt.

Beachte:

Das indirekte Objekt muss im Passivsatz mit *to* angeschlossen werden.

G 24

Passiv → Aktiv

- Der mit *by* angeschlossene Handelnde *(by-agent)* des Passivsatzes wird zum Subjekt des Aktivsatzes; *by* entfällt.
- Das Subjekt des Passivsatzes wird zum Objekt des Aktivsatzes.
- Fehlt im Passivsatz der *by-agent*, muss im Aktivsatz ein Handelnder als Subjekt ergänzt werden, z. B. *somebody, we, you, they.*

Passiv: The milk   is bought   by Joe.
        Subjekt   *by-agent*

Aktiv: Joe   buys   the milk.
     Subjekt   *Objekt*

Passiv: The match   was won.
        Subjekt

Aktiv: They   won   the match.
     (ergänztes)   *Objekt*
     Subjekt

Der Satz im Englischen

12 Wortstellung – *Word Order*

Im Aussagesatz gilt die Wortstellung Subjekt – Prädikat – Objekt *(subject – verb – object):*

- Subjekt: Wer oder was tut etwas?
- Prädikat: Was wird getan?
- Objekt: Worauf / Auf wen bezieht sich die Tätigkeit?

Für die Position von Orts- und Zeitangaben vgl. S. G 4 f.

Cats catch mice.
Katzen fangen Mäuse.

13 Konditionalsätze – *Conditional Sentences*

Ein Konditionalsatz (Bedingungssatz) besteht aus zwei Teilen: einem Nebensatz *(if-clause)* und einem Hauptsatz *(main clause)*. Im *if*-Satz steht die **Bedingung** *(condition)*, unter der die im **Hauptsatz** genannte **Folge** eintritt. Man unterscheidet drei Arten von Konditionalsätzen:

Konditionalsatz Typ I

Bildung

- *if*-Satz (Bedingung):
  simple present

  If you <u>read</u> this book,
  Wenn du dieses Buch liest,

- Hauptsatz (Folge):
  will-future

  you <u>will learn</u> a lot about music.
  erfährst du eine Menge über Musik.

Der *if*-Satz kann auch nach dem Hauptsatz stehen. In diesem Fall entfällt das Komma:

- Hauptsatz: *will-future*

  You <u>will learn</u> a lot about music
  Du erfährst eine Menge über Musik,

- *if*-Satz: *simple present*

  <u>if</u> you <u>read</u> this book.
  wenn du dieses Buch liest.

Im Hauptsatz kann auch

- *can* + Infinitiv,

  If you go to London, you <u>can</u> <u>see</u> Bob.
  Wenn du nach London fährst, kannst du Bob treffen.

- *must* + Infinitiv,

  If you go to London, you <u>must</u> <u>visit</u> me.
  Wenn du nach London fährst, musst du mich besuchen.

- der Imperativ

  stehen.

  If it rains, <u>take</u> an umbrella.
  Wenn es regnet, nimm einen Schirm mit.

Verwendung
Bedingungssätze vom Typ I verwendet man, wenn die **Bedingung erfüllbar** ist. Man gibt an, was unter bestimmten Bedingungen **geschieht** oder **geschehen kann**.

Konditionalsatz Typ II

Bildung

- *if*-Satz (Bedingung):
  simple past

  If I <u>went</u> to London,
  Wenn ich nach London fahren würde,

- Hauptsatz (Folge):
  conditional I = would + Infinitiv

  I <u>would</u> <u>visit</u> the Tower.
  würde ich mir den Tower ansehen.

Verwendung

Bedingungssätze vom Typ II verwendet man, wenn die **Bedingung nur theoretisch erfüllt** werden kann oder **nicht erfüllbar** ist.

Konditionalsatz Typ III

Bildung

- *if*-Satz (Bedingung): *past perfect*

  If I had gone to London,
  Wenn ich nach London gefahren wäre,

- Hauptsatz (Folge): *conditional II = would + have + past participle*

  I would have visited the Tower of London.
  hätte ich mir den Tower of London angesehen.

Verwendung

Bedingungssätze vom Typ III verwendet man, wenn sich die **Bedingung auf die Vergangenheit bezieht** und deshalb **nicht mehr erfüllbar** ist.

14 Relativsätze – *Relative Clauses*

Ein Relativsatz ist ein Nebensatz, der sich **auf eine Person oder Sache** des Hauptsatzes **bezieht** und diese **näher beschreibt**:

- Hauptsatz:
- Relativsatz:

The boy who looks like Jane is her brother.
Der Junge, der Jane ähnlich sieht, ist ihr Bruder.

The boy ... is her brother.
... who looks like Jane ...

Bildung

Haupt- und Nebensatz werden durch das Relativpronomen verbunden.

- *who* (Nominativ oder Akkusativ),

Peter, who lives in London, likes travelling.
Peter, der in London lebt, reist gerne.

G 27

whose (Genitiv) und

whom (Akkusativ) beziehen sich auf **Personen**,

- *which* bezieht sich auf **Sachen**,

- *that* kann sich auf **Sachen** und auf **Personen** beziehen und wird nur verwendet, wenn die **Information** im Relativsatz **notwendig** ist, um den ganzen Satz zu verstehen.

Sam, <u>whose</u> mother is an architect, is in my class.
Sam, dessen Mutter Architektin ist, geht in meine Klasse.
Anne, <u>whom</u>/<u>who</u> I like very much, is French.
Anne, die ich sehr mag, ist Französin.
The film "Dark Moon", <u>which</u> we saw yesterday, was far too long.
Der Film „Dark Moon", den wir gestern sahen, war viel zu lang.
The film <u>that</u> we saw last week was much better.
Der Film, den wir letzte Woche sahen, war viel besser.

Verwendung
Mithilfe von Relativpronomen kann man **zwei Sätze miteinander verbinden**.

<u>London</u> is England's biggest city. <u>London</u> has about 7.2 million inhabitants.
London ist Englands größte Stadt. London hat etwa 7,2 Millionen Einwohner.

London, <u>which</u> is England's biggest city, has about 7.2 million inhabitants.
London, die größte Stadt Englands, hat etwa 7,2 Millionen Einwohner.

Beachte:
Man unterscheidet zwei Arten von Relativsätzen:
- **Notwendige Relativsätze** (*defining relative clauses*) enthalten Informationen, die **für das Verständnis** des Satzes **erforderlich** sind.

  Hier kann das Relativpronomen entfallen, wenn es Objekt ist; man spricht dann auch von *contact clauses*.

The man <u>who is wearing a red shirt</u> is Mike.
Der Mann, der ein rotes Hemd trägt, ist Mike.

The book (<u>that</u>) I bought yesterday is thrilling.
Das Buch, das ich gestern gekauft habe, ist spannend.

- **Nicht notwendige Relativsätze** (*non-defining relative clauses*) enthalten **zusätzliche Informationen** zum Bezugswort, die für das Verständnis des Satzes nicht unbedingt notwendig sind. Dieser Typ von Relativsatz wird **mit Komma** abgetrennt.

Sally, who went to a party yesterday, is very tired.
Sally, die gestern auf einer Party war, ist sehr müde.

15 Indirekte Rede – *Reported Speech*

Die indirekte Rede verwendet man, um **wiederzugeben, was ein anderer gesagt** oder **gefragt hat.**

Bildung
Um die indirekte Rede zu bilden, benötigt man ein **Einleitungsverb.**
Häufig verwendete Einleitungsverben sind:

to say, to tell, to add, to mention, to think, to ask, to want to know, to answer

In der indirekten Rede verändern sich die **Pronomen**, in bestimmten Fällen auch die **Zeiten** und die **Orts-** und **Zeitangaben.**

- Wie die Pronomen sich verändern, hängt vom jeweiligen **Kontext** ab.

direkte Rede	indirekte Rede
Bob says to Jenny: "I like you."	Jenny tells Liz: "Bob says that he likes me."
Bob sagt zu Jenny: „Ich mag dich."	*Jenny erzählt Liz: „Bob sagt, dass er mich mag."*
Aber:	Jenny tells Liz that Bob likes her.
	Jenny erzählt Liz, dass Bob sie mag.

- **Zeiten:**
  Keine Veränderung, wenn das Einleitungsverb im *simple present* oder im *present perfect* steht:

direkte Rede	indirekte Rede
Bob says, "I love dancing."	Bob says (that) he loves dancing.
Bob sagt: „Ich tanze sehr gerne."	*Bob sagt, er tanze sehr gerne.*

In folgenden Fällen wird die Zeit der direkten Rede in der indirekten Rede **um eine Zeitstufe zurückversetzt**, wenn das **Einleitungsverb** im *simple past* steht:

simple present	→	*simple past*
simple past	→	*past perfect*
present perfect	→	*past perfect*
will-future	→	*conditional I*

- **Zeitangaben** verändern sich, wenn der Bericht zu einem späteren Zeitpunkt erfolgt, z. B.:
- Welche **Ortsangabe** verwendet wird, hängt davon ab, wo sich der Sprecher im Moment befindet.

Bob said, "I love dancing."
Bob sagte: „Ich tanze sehr gerne. "

Bob said (that) he loved dancing.
Bob sagte, er tanze sehr gerne.

Joe: "I like it."
Joe: "I liked it."
Joe: "I've liked it."
Joe: "I will like it."

Joe said he liked it.
Joe said he had liked it.
Joe said he had liked it.
Joe said he would like it.

now	→	then, at that time
today	→	that day, yesterday
yesterday	→	the day before
the day before yesterday	→	two days before
tomorrow	→	the following day
next week	→	the following week
here	→	there

Bildung der indirekten Frage
Häufige Einleitungsverben für die indirekte Frage sind:

to ask, to want to know, to wonder

- **Fragewörter** bleiben in der indirekten Rede **erhalten**. Die **Umschreibung** mit *do/does/did* **entfällt** in der indirekten Frage.

Tom: "When did they arrive?"
Tom: „Wann sind sie angekommen?"

Tom asked when they had arrived.
Tom fragte, wann sie angekommen seien.

- Enthält die direkte Frage **kein Fragewort**, wird die indirekte Frage mit *whether* oder *if* eingeleitet:

Tom: "Are they staying at the hotel?"

Tom: „Übernachten sie im Hotel?"

Tom asked if/ whether they were staying at the hotel.

Tom fragte, ob sie im Hotel übernachten.

Befehle/Aufforderungen in der indirekten Rede
Häufige Einleitungsverben sind:

to tell, to order, to ask

In der indirekten Rede steht hier **Einleitungsverb + Objekt + (not) to + Infinitiv**.

Tom: "Leave the room."
Tom: „Verlass den Raum. "

Tom told me to leave the room.
Tom forderte mich auf, den Raum zu verlassen.

Anhang

16 Liste wichtiger unregelmäßiger Verben – *List of Irregular Verbs*

Infinitive	Simple Past	Past Participle	*Deutsch*
be	was/were	been	*sein*
begin	began	begun	*beginnen*
blow	blew	blown	*wehen, blasen*
break	broke	broken	*brechen*
bring	brought	brought	*bringen*
build	built	built	*bauen*
buy	bought	bought	*kaufen*
catch	caught	caught	*fangen*
choose	chose	chosen	*wählen*
come	came	come	*kommen*
cut	cut	cut	*schneiden*
do	did	done	*tun*
draw	drew	drawn	*zeichnen*
drink	drank	drunk	*trinken*
drive	drove	driven	*fahren*
eat	ate	eaten	*essen*
fall	fell	fallen	*fallen*
feed	fed	fed	*füttern*
feel	felt	felt	*fühlen*
find	found	found	*finden*
fly	flew	flown	*fliegen*
get	got	got	*bekommen*
give	gave	given	*geben*
go	went	gone	*gehen*
grow	grew	grown	*wachsen*
hang	hung	hung	*hängen*
have	had	had	*haben*
hear	heard	heard	*hören*
hit	hit	hit	*schlagen*
hold	held	held	*halten*
keep	kept	kept	*halten*
know	knew	known	*wissen*

Infinitive	Simple Past	Past Participle	*Deutsch*
lay	laid	laid	*legen*
leave	left	left	*verlassen*
let	let	let	*lassen*
lie	lay	lain	*liegen*
lose	lost	lost	*verlieren*
make	made	made	*machen*
meet	met	met	*treffen*
pay	paid	paid	*bezahlen*
put	put	put	*stellen/setzen*
read	read	read	*lesen*
ring	rang	rung	*läuten/anrufen*
run	ran	run	*rennen*
say	said	said	*sagen*
see	saw	seen	*sehen*
send	sent	sent	*schicken*
show	showed	shown	*zeigen*
sing	sang	sung	*singen*
sit	sat	sat	*sitzen*
sleep	slept	slept	*schlafen*
smell	smelt	smelt	*riechen*
speak	spoke	spoken	*sprechen*
spend	spent	spent	*ausgeben/ verbringen*
stand	stood	stood	*stehen*
steal	stole	stolen	*stehlen*
swim	swam	swum	*schwimmen*
take	took	taken	*nehmen*
teach	taught	taught	*lehren*
tell	told	told	*erzählen*
think	thought	thought	*denken*
throw	threw	thrown	*werfen*
wake	woke	woken	*aufwachen*
wear	wore	worn	*tragen*
win	won	won	*gewinnen*
write	wrote	written	*schreiben*

Original-Prüfungsaufgaben

Erster Prüfungsteil: Hörverstehen

Aufgabe 1: Selektives Verstehen: *London attractions*

The Southall family is on holiday in London. They are calling different information hotlines. You are going to hear the hotlines they are calling.

> - *First read the example (0) and the statements (1–10).*
> - *Then listen to the hotlines.*
> - *Complete the statements while you are listening.*
> - *At the end you will hear the hotlines again.*
> - *Now read the example (0) and the statements (1–10). You have 60 seconds to do this.*

Now listen to the hotlines and complete the statements (1–10).

Example (0):   The **Tower of London** is closed after __6 p.m.__ .

1. At **Windsor Castle** some of the rooms are closed for visitors after _____ September.

2. If you buy a child's ticket for **The London Eye**, you pay half the price for a _____ one.

3. **Madame Tussauds** wax museum is closed on _____.

4. You can get refreshments in **Whipsnade Wild Animal Park**'s _____.

5. If you book your ticket for **Chessington World of Adventures and Zoo** online, the family ticket costs only £ _____.

6. **Wycombe Chair Museum** is closed on _____ and bank holidays.

7. At **The London Dungeons** you can learn about London's violent and dangerous _____.

8. The pools at the **London Aquarium** contain more than _____ of water.

9. You should book in advance to get a ticket for a guided tour of not more than _____ people at **Kew Gardens**.

10. The best and easiest way to go to the **O2 Arena** is by _____.

Aufgabe 2: Detailliertes Verstehen: *Choosing a school*

You are going to hear a dialogue. Sally, an English student of Australian history, wants to study abroad. She's talking to her professor to get further information.

- *First read the tasks (1–10).*
- *Then listen to the dialogue.*
- *Tick the correct box for each task while you are listening.*
- *Tick only **one** box for each task.*
- *At the end you will hear the dialogue again.*
- *Now read the tasks (1–10). You have 2 minutes to do this.*

Now listen to the dialogue and tick the correct box for each task (1–10).

1. The programme is organized by …
    a) ☐ a professor from Sydney University.
    b) ☐ the Centre of Australian History.
    c) ☐ the Sydney City Council.

2. The campus is …
    a) ☐ a fifteen minute walk from the city centre.
    b) ☐ in the city centre.
    c) ☐ located in a quiet suburb.

3. The centre is run …
    a) ☐ by a government organisation.
    b) ☐ by Sydney authorities.
    c) ☐ privately.

4. The programme offers a stay of …
    a) ☐ eight weeks only.
    b) ☐ longer than twelve weeks.
    c) ☐ up to twelve weeks.

5. Professor Smith thinks the length of the programme is …
    a) ☐ just right.
    b) ☐ too long.
    c) ☐ too short.

6. In a class there are …
    a) ☐ ten to fifteen students.
    b) ☐ twenty to thirty students.
    c) ☐ usually not more than ten students.

7. In summer there are …
   a) ☐ different possibilities.
   b) ☐ only larger classes.
   c) ☐ only private classes.

8. According to Professor Smith …
   a) ☐ both class sizes have advantages.
   b) ☐ larger classes are more effective.
   c) ☐ smaller classes are less effective.

9. On campus you can live …
   a) ☐ alone in a flat.
   b) ☐ in a large dorm.
   c) ☐ with another student.

10. Home stays …
    a) ☐ are not offered.
    b) ☐ are organized by the school.
    c) ☐ must be organized by the students themselves.

Aufgabe 3: Globales Verstehen: *Australian cities* 💿

You are going to hear a radio programme called "The Lost Outback" with John and Kevin. They are discussing the advantages and disadvantages of six Australian cities.

- *First read the statements (A–G) and look at the list of cities (0–5).*
- *Then listen to the programme.*
- *Choose the correct statement for each city and write the letters in the correct boxes.*
- *There is an **example** at the **beginning (0)**.*
- *There is one more statement than you need.*
- *At the end you will hear the programme again.*
- *Now read the statements (A–G). You have 30 seconds to do this.*

Now listen to the programme and choose the correct statement (A–G) for each city (1–5).
This Australian city is a really great place for people who love …

A	a place near the dry outback.
B	a city centre by a river.
C	beautiful nature nearby.
D	**a fantastic harbour.**
E	dangerous wildlife.
F	street markets.
G	cultural life in a big city.

Example – 0 Sydney	**D**
1 Melbourne	
2 Brisbane	
3 Adelaide	
4 Perth	
5 Darwin	

Zweiter Prüfungsteil: Wortschatz – Leseverstehen – Schreiben

Aufgabe 4: *Lost in the Australian bush*

4.1 Wortschatz

This text (sentences 1–13) is about a group of young people who took part in a survival course in the Australian outback.

- *Sentences 1, 3, 5, 8, 10, 13: Tick the correct box (there is only **one** correct answer).*
- *Sentences 2, 4, 6, 7, 9, 11, 12: Fill in suitable words.*

1. Many teenagers think Australia is a great place to go. They …
   a) ☐ learn   b) ☐ like
   c) ☐ listen   d) ☐ teach
   about this in school,

2. The teenagers were told that finding water is the most _____ thing to do in the bush.

3. One rule is that if you want to go for a walk, you should always leave a …
   a) ☐ leaflet.   b) ☐ message.
   c) ☐ paper.   d) ☐ report.

4. It is not easy to _____ with problems like hunger and loneliness.

2010-4

5. During the survival trip they were taught how to live …
   a) ☐ at
   b) ☐ by
   c) ☐ on
   d) ☐ with
   leaves and seeds.

6. The Aboriginal guide showed them his boomerang. He used it to _____ small animals.

7. The native people of Australia know how to _____ in the outback.

8. Some of the teenagers were really …
   a) ☐ frightening
   b) ☐ scared
   c) ☐ scary
   d) ☐ thrilling
   because they had to sleep outside.

9. "A lot of people dream of adventurous trips in the outback, but many of them don't _____ how dangerous it really is", said the guide.

10. a) ☐ Although
    b) ☐ Because
    c) ☐ Besides
    d) ☐ Even
    … one should not forget that Australia is the home of many dangerous animals.

11. Learning what to do in the outback is sometimes really hard so that three teenagers felt extremely _____ after the first two days.

12. "On such trips you can learn a lot about _____ you can use to survive", one of the teenagers said.

13. For rescue teams it can be …
    a) ☐ rare
    b) ☐ regular
    c) ☐ ridiculous
    d) ☐ risky
    to search for people who are lost in the outback.

4.2 Leseverstehen

The following text is about a teenager who went on a walk and got lost.

> - *First read the text.*
> - *Then do the tasks (1–6)*

Lost in the Australian bush

July 16, 2009, by Victoria Ward

1　A British teenager lost in the Australian bush for twelve days said last night: "That was a nightmare. I was so scared. I still can't believe that everything is over now."

　　Jamie Neale, 18, from London, was miraculously[1] found alive and well by 5 two Australian walkers. When his father saw him in hospital he said: "He's the only teenager in the world who goes on a 10-mile walk and leaves his mobile phone behind."

　　Jamie went for a walk in the Blue Mountains, about two hours inland from Sydney, a popular place for tourists who like adventures, with dense eucalyptus 10 bushland and rainforests.

　　"I was so excited", he told us, "I wanted to see koalas, wombats and kangaroos in their native environment."

　　He was reported missing when he failed to turn up for a pre-booked tour of some nearby caves the following day.

15　After two days his bottle of water was empty and the dried fruits were eaten.

　　He survived because he ate seeds, leaves and lettuce-like plants. Sometimes he even dug for earthworms. At night he slept by huddling up in his jacket and on one night under a log[2]. A 400-strong search team started to look for him using helicopters and dogs, as well as police, fire brigade officers, park rangers and 20 emergency service volunteers.

　　Jamie's dad Richard flew out to join the massive search operation. He always believed in the success of the operation.

　　Officer Denis Clifford said it was "like searching for a needle in a haystack".

　　As Jamie stumbled around trying to find his way out, sipping rainwater from 25 leaves, he could hear the sounds of a rescue helicopter in the distance. But his desperate calls for help went unheard. He told his dad he had walked up to higher ground to get some orientation but lost his way back in the trees.

　　He remembered: "I was scared they'd stop looking for me. I could see the helicopters flying overhead but they couldn't see me." But then, two Aussie 30 bushwalkers luckily stumbled upon the teenager yesterday.

　　One had medical experience and treated Jamie on a mountain track before he was taken to hospital.

A text message was sent to Jamie's father. It said 'Phone me, I've got good news.'

35 "That was when I knew he was safe. It was absolutely stunning. I was at the hotel, surrounded by strangers. 'My boy's been found, my boy's been found!' I shouted."

Mum Jean Neale insisted: "I never gave up hope. You never give up hope on your children. As far as I was concerned, he was coming home. I told all the
40 family and his friends that he was coming home and I had no doubts³ about that. That kept them strong and in turn that kept me strong."

The parents were relieved⁴ and they told the reporters:

"If he goes travelling again, we will get one of those watches with a GPS so he can be picked up if he goes walkabout again. He's not leaving the country
45 again until he has got one of those."

based on DailyRecord.co.uk vom 16. Juli 2009

Annotations
1 miraculously – *wie durch ein Wunder*
2 log – big piece of wood
3 doubts – *Zweifel*
4 relieved – *erleichtert*

- *Now read the following tasks carefully.*
- *Tick the correct box for each task. Tick only **one** box for each task.*

1. The rescue of the British teenager was …
   a) ☐ a nightmare.
   b) ☐ an unexpected surprise.
   c) ☐ possible because of his mobile.
   d) ☐ scary.

2. The Blue Mountains are …
   a) ☐ a dangerous place because of the koalas.
   b) ☐ a desert-like place near Sydney.
   c) ☐ a well-known tourist attraction.
   d) ☐ popular because of the natives.

3. Jamie survived because he …
   a) ☐ found a log.
   b) ☐ had a bottle of water.
   c) ☐ had enough food in his rucksack.
   d) ☐ was able to find food.

4. Finally, Jamie was rescued because …
   a) ☐ he shouted desperately.
   b) ☐ he was found by chance.
   c) ☐ helicopters were used.
   d) ☐ his father helped to find him.

5. After Jamie's rescue his father …
   a) ☐ received a message.
   b) ☐ was given a telephone.
   c) ☐ was informed by the hospital.
   d) ☐ was phoned at the hotel.

6. His parents want him to …
   a) ☐ leave the country.
   b) ☐ stop going for walks.
   c) ☐ travel to other countries.
   d) ☐ wear a special watch.

4.3 Schreiben

- *Read the tasks carefully.*
- *Write complete sentences.*
- *Make sure to write about **all** the aspects presented in each task.*

1. Describe in detail Jamie's strategy to survive in the bush **and** the actions taken to rescue him.

2. Describe what Jamie's parents think and feel **before** and **after** the rescue of their son and explain their reactions.

3. You have a choice here. Choose **one** of the following tasks:

   a) Do **you** think it is good for young people to go on adventure trips like Jamie? Find arguments for and against such trips and express your personal opinion.

   or

   b) Imagine you are Jamie. Back home in London you are asked to write an article for a school magazine. Write about the risks of such a trip and give some tips on how to be really well prepared.

Erster Prüfungsteil: Hörverstehen

Mittlerer Schulabschluss – Haupttermin

Wichtige Hinweise: Alle Texte, die du im Folgenden hörst, werden zweimal vorgespielt. Vor dem ersten Hören hast du Zeit, dich mit den Aufgaben vertraut zu machen. Der Hörverstehenstest besteht aus drei Teilen.

Aufgabe 1: Selektives Verstehen – *London attractions*

The Southall family is on holiday in London. They are calling different informa-tion hotlines. You are going to hear the hotlines they are calling.

First read the example (0) and the statements 1–10. Then listen to the hotlines. Complete the statements while you are listening. At the end you will hear the hotlines again. Now read the example (0) and the statements 1–10. You have sixty seconds to do this.

(60 seconds' break)

Now listen to the hotlines and complete the statements 1–10.

1 Mr Southall phones the first hotline and listens to the following announcement:
   *Welcome to the **Tower of London** booking line. Come and visit one of the most popular sights in London. It is one of the most visited museums in London. In the summer we are open daily from 10 a.m. to 6 p.m. From Tuesday to Satur-*
5 *day we open at 9 a.m. Last admission is at 5 p.m.*

   Then Mr Southall dials the next number:
   *Welcome to **Windsor Castle**. It is the oldest and largest occupied castle in the world, and the official residence of Queen Elizabeth II. Take advantage while you can – the State rooms are only open to the public until Saturday 26th Sep-*
10 *tember! Open daily from 9.45 until 5.15. Prices start from £ 8 ...*

   Then his daughter Rachel listens to the next announcement:
   *Welcome to **The London Eye**, the experience for young and old on the bank of the River Thames next to Waterloo Station. Check out our special offers for May! Buy one child's ticket – and get the second half price! Terms and conditions*
15 *apply. Call our ticket hotline on ...*

After that Rachel phones Madame Tussauds:

*Visit **Madame Tussauds in London** – the world's most famous wax museum. Come face-to-face with stars such as David Beckham, Barack Obama and many, many others! Madame Tussauds is very accessible – the closest underground* 20 *station is Baker Street. Open every day except Christmas Day. Visit the museum's homepage www...*

Then Rachel listens to a short audio file on the Internet:

***Whipsnade Wild Animal Park** offers a fantastic family day out. Get up close with a variety of animals. Let the kids run wild in our adventure playground! For* 25 *an even better experience, take advantage of our wonderful restaurants and bars. We could even host your wedding! Whipsnade Wild Animal Park – open from March to October – Ticket prices ...*

The Southalls listen to another announcement:

***Chessington World of Adventures and Zoo**! Open every day from 10 a.m.* 30 *until 6 p.m. New for 2009 – two brand new restaurants. Take advantage of our online discount – £78 for a family ticket when you book online – a great saving of £14! For more information visit our website.*

They go on phoning hotlines:

*Thank you for calling the **Wycombe Chair Museum** information hotline. The* 35 *museum is open from Monday to Saturday from 9.30 a.m. until 3.30 p.m., but not on Sundays or bank holidays. Adult tickets are £4, and child tickets £2. There are no family tickets. For more information, please visit our website.*

Rachel remembers a rather different sort of attraction and asks her father to phone it:

40 *Uuuuaaarrrggghh! This is **The London Dungeons** – discover more about London's violent and dangerous past! Visit the darkest chapters of London's history. Only £15 per person – strictly over 18s only. For more information, call ...*

Rachel's brother Thomas dials another hotline:

*The **London Aquarium** is located in Westminster on the bank of the river* 45 *Thames right in the heart of London. Only ten minutes from the London Eye, It is one of the world's largest aquariums, containing over 1 million litres of water! It is also the only place in Britain where you can see seven different species of shark. To book tickets call 0800 12 ...*

Then Mrs Southall listens to the following announcement:

50 **Kew Gardens** *is one of the world's leading botanic gardens. Open daily from 9.30 till sunset. This summer, Kew celebrates its 250th anniversary, with many spectacular events, including 'The Power of Plants' tour, every day at 12 noon limited to 15 people per tour. So make sure you book in advance. Adult prices only …*

55 After that Thomas listens to another announcement:

London's O2 Arena *is a fantastic venue for concerts. This year, see Britney Spears, Pink and Green Day perform live! London's O2 Arena is a fantastic venue for sports events, shows, such as comedian Al Murray and 'Disney on Ice'. London's O2 Arena is easy to get to by tube – take the Jubilee Line to North* 60 *Greenwich.*

Now listen to the hotlines again and check your answers.

1. 26/26th
   ✓ **Hinweis:** *"Take advantage while you can – the State rooms are only open to the public until Saturday 26th September!" (Z. 8 ff.)*

2. second
   ✓ **Hinweis:** *"Buy one child's ticket – and get the second half price!" (Z. 14)*

3. Christmas Day
   ✓ **Hinweis:** *"Open every day except Christmas Day" (Z. 20)*

4. restaurants and bars/bars, restaurants
   ✓ **Hinweis:** *"For an even better experience, take advantage of our wonderful restaurants and bars." (Z. 24 ff.)*

5. 78/seventy-eight
   ✓ **Hinweis:** *"Take advantage of our online discount – £ 78 for a family ticket when you book online" (Z. 30 f.)*

6. Sundays
   ✓ **Hinweis:** *"The museum is open from Monday to Saturday from 9:30 a.m. until 3:30 p.m., but not on Sundays or bank holidays."(Z. 34 ff.)*

7. past/history/times
   ✓ **Hinweis:** *"… discover more about London's violent and dangerous past! Visit the darkest chapters of London's history." (Z. 40 ff.)*

8. one million litres/1,000,000 litres
   Hinweis: "*It is one of the world's largest aquariums, containing over 1 million litres of water*" (Z. 45 f.)

9. 15/fifteen
   Hinweis: "*… including 'The Power of Plants' tour, every day at 12 noon limited to 15 people per tour.*" (Z. 52 f.)

10. tube/underground/subway
   Hinweis: "*London's O2 Arena is easy to get to by tube …*" (Z. 59)

Aufgabe 2: Detailliertes Verstehen – *Choosing a school*

> *You are going to hear a dialogue. Sally, an English student of Australian history, wants to study abroad. She's talking to her professor to get further information.*
>
> *First read the tasks 1–10. Then listen to the dialogue. Tick the correct box for each task while you are listening. Tick only one box for each task. At the end you will hear the dialogue again. Now read the tasks 1–10. You have two minutes to do this.* (2 minutes' break)
>
> *Now listen to the dialogue and tick the correct box for each task 1–10.*

1 PROFESSOR: Good afternoon, Sally. I'm glad to hear you're interested in studying abroad for some time.

SALLY: Yes, thank you for meeting me, Professor Smith. I'm really interested in studying Down Under. I'd appreciate any information you can give me about
5 the programme there.

PROFESSOR: Well, the programme in Australia is offered by the Centre of Australian History near Sydney.

SALLY: Sydney? Wow! Is the school downtown?

PROFESSOR: Actually the Campus is about fifteen minutes from downtown Sydney
10 by train. It's located in a small residential area which is quiet and convenient – perfect for a student.

SALLY: Err … can you tell me what type of school the Centre is?

PROFESSOR: Sure, the Centre's rather small. It's run by a private organisation with a staff of about eight or ten teachers. That's something to consider care-
15 fully. At a small school like that you won't have as many chances to meet Australian students, not like you would at a large university.

SALLY: How long is the programme? Can you tell me how long students usually study there?

PROFESSOR: Err … well, for the length of stay the Centre offers two choices.
20   Students can stay either eight or twelve weeks. Unfortunately they don't
have any longer programme options. Now, some people may disagree, but
personally, I think students need much more time to really learn about the
Aboriginal languages and their culture.

SALLY: Right.

25 PROFESSOR: OK. Err … let's move to class size. As you know the Centre's a
small school, so the classes are mainly small. The average class size is five
to ten students, but there are also larger classes, especially in the winter term.
That's when many foreign students like you attend the school. Erm … I'm
not sure, but I think in the summer they also offer private classes for students
30   who are interested in studying just one-to-one with a teacher.

SALLY: Err … Professor Smith, do you think a small class is better than a large
class?

PROFESSOR: Yeah, good question. With small group or private classes, you really
have a chance to learn rather individually, which means, of course, more ef-
35   fectively. I think in large classes, the improvement can take longer, but on
the other hand you get to know other students and you can exchange experiences with them. Err, is there anything else you wanted to know about,
Sally?

SALLY: Yes, can you tell me what kind of housing is available?

40 PROFESSOR: The school has a small dorm located next to the school building.
You'd be in a room with a student from another country, or possibly also
from the same country. You can also rent an apartment in town, if you prefer.

SALLY: How about a home stay? Can I do that?

PROFESSOR: Yes, err … the school can also match you with a home stay family
45   and arrange the details of the home stay for you. For studying abroad I think
it's important to have a lot of options.

SALLY: Wow! It sounds great. Thanks very much for your help, Professor Smith.

PROFESSOR: You're welcome, Sally, and good luck! I'm sure you'll have a great
time abroad.

Now listen to the dialogue again and check your answers.

---

1.   b) … the Centre of Australian History.
    Hinweis: *"Well, the programme in Australia is offered by the Centre of
Australian History near Sydney." (Z. 6 f.)*

2.   c) … located in a quiet suburb.
    Hinweis: *"It's located in a small residential area which is quiet and
convenient …" (Z. 10)*

3. c) ... privately.
   / **Hinweis::** *"It's run by a private organization ..." (Z. 13)*

4. c) ... up to twelve weeks.
   / **Hinweis:** *"Students can stay either eight or twelve weeks. Unfortunately they don't have any longer programme options." (Z. 20f.)*

5. c) ... too short.
   / **Hinweis:** *"... I think students need much more time to really learn about the Aboriginal languages and their culture." (Z. 22f.)*

6. c) ... usually not more than ten students.
   / **Hinweis:** *"The average class size is five to ten students ..." (Z. 26f.)*

7. a) ... different possibilities.
   / **Hinweis:** *"... I think in the summer they also offer private classes for students who are interested in studying just one-to-one ..." (Z. 29f.)*

8. a) ... both class sizes have advantages.
   / **Hinweis:** *"... With small group or private classes, you really have a chance to learn rather individually, which means, of course, more effectively. I think in large classes, the improvement can take longer, but on the other hand you get to know other students and you can exchange experiences with them ..." (Z. 33ff.)*

9. c) ... with another student.
   / **Hinweis:** *"You'd be in a room with a student from another country, or possibly also from the same country." (Z. 41f.)*

10. b) ... are organized by the school.
    / **Hinweis:** *"... the school can also match you with a home stay family and arrange the details of the home stay for you." (Z. 44f.)*

Aufgabe 3: Globales Verstehen: *Australian cities*

> *You are going to hear a radio programme called "The Lost Outback" with John and Kevin. They are discussing the advantages and disadvantages of six Australian cities. First read the statements A–G and look at the list of cities 0–5. Then listen to the programme. Choose the correct statement for each city and write the letters in the correct boxes. There is an example at the beginning (0). There is one more statement than you need. At the end you will hear the programme again. Now read the statements A–G. You have thirty seconds to do this. (30 seconds' break)*
> *Now listen to the programme and choose the correct statement A–G for each city 1–5.*

KEVIN: Hi there and welcome to the Lost Outback podcast. I'm Kevin.

JOHN: Yes and my name is John.

KEVIN: We're your two outsiders on the inside.

JOHN: Yes, yes, telling you all you don't need to know about Australia. Actually, this week, we actually do have something very useful to talk about. We've actually put a bit of thought into this episode.

KEVIN: Yes, it's once around Australia. We, we've thought of all of you people who are thinking about coming to Australia for a holiday or even to live and ... err ... the first choice you have to make is which of Australia's big cities are you gonna land in.

JOHN: So, so, we're doing a virtual tour. Alright Kevin, where are we going to first?

KEVIN: We're gonna start in Sydney because it's the only city in Australia that many people in the world have heard of.

JOHN: A few things going for it. It's got the, the harbour and kind of the waterfront on the harbour and it's got, err, behind that, err, the beaches and they're incredible as well, too. But it's, it's, kind of the, the thing with Sydney is, it's got this amazing piece of water and then there's nothing really behind it.

KEVIN: That's right. I've been ... I've heard ... err ... tell that if you took the ... erm ... harbour out of Sydney, there would be no redeeming qualities left to the place. So Sydney is in New South Wales, which is kind of a rather large southeastern state. And so from Sydney I'd like to go ... err ... south to Melbourne in ... err ... the state of Victoria.

JOHN: Melbourne has really bad weather but it has really, really good ... err ... indoor culture because of that.

KEVIN: I wouldn't say it has really bad weather. For Australia maybe but ...

JOHN: For Australia it has bad weather.

KEVIN: ... for the rest of the world. You're never gonna get snow in Melbourne. That's a plus. But the thing that Melbourne has, as with a lot of Australia, is unpredictable weather. You can have a sunny, beautiful day and then suddenly – whoosh – this wind picks up and you're ... carrying you down the street.

KEVIN: So Melbourne is still quite a big city and you, you'll, you'll have all the big city amenities but it's not as big as Sydney and ... err ... it's not as crowded as Sydney and, and I find it's, it's more cultural. It's got more of a cultural identity as, as a city. Erm ... and, err ... yeah, great place to come and live. Moving on to Brisbane which is ... err ... north of Sydney along the coast. Erm ... a lot of people think of it as a very northern ... err ... city because it's like a holiday destination. It's bright and sunny and, and ... almost tropical but I think it is still sub-tropical.

JOHN: Yeah, it's, yeah ... I believe it is.

KEVIN: OK, so Brisbane is ... err ... Australia's fastest growing city as I understand it. This is what I've been told. Erm ... it's a river city. It's got this river
that goes right through the centre of the city. And ... so, there's a lot of
bridges going over that. And there is a lot of boat activity on, on the river.
OK, we're moving along to Adelaide.
JOHN: Actually it's right on the doorstep of the desert.
KEVIN: Oh!
JOHN: So you, you go about maybe, erm ... you know, 50 ks or so out of Ade-
laide, maybe even 25 ks out of Adelaide, and it really begins to get quite
arid.
KEVIN: That's right.
JOHN: And ...
KEVIN: And they just put in a great, big train line that goes north from Adelaide
straight into the centre of Australia to ... erm ... Alice Springs.
JOHN: OK, so Kevin, where are we off to now?
KEVIN: Erm ... I think we have to head over to the west coast of Australia. And
that's Perth. The only difference is that Perth is the only big city on the west
coast of Australia.
JOHN: So, it's in the middle of nowhere.
KEVIN: It's a popular ... err ... vacation spot for people who live in the rest of
Australia. They wanna go and see some place new but not necessarily fly
overseas for a really expensive time. Erm ... yeah, it's got a lot of stuff
around it to go see as far as natural environment.
JOHN: Yeah ...
KEVIN: You can go out into the desert and you can go down along the coast to
the beaches. Lots of stuff to see.
JOHN: And ... it's ... The beaches are ... It is famous for its beaches. It's got
these kilometres of beaches that go as far as the eye can see. And they're just
pristine. And there's also a ... a very good wine ... err ... growing regions
around Perth as well.
KEVIN: So it's got a bit of everything, Perth. OK. We've got Darwin in the
Northern Territories which is really hot half of the year and really raining the
other half of the year, yeah
JOHN: ... the other half of the year, yeah; it really is kind of crocodiles and
snakes and ...
KEVIN: Yeah, it's Australia's jungle city.
JOHN: Yeah, it is ...
KEVIN: Err ..., so, you know, check it out if you're hardcore but otherwise I'd
say, stay away.
JOHN: And it's ... it's not very big. It's got a population, I think, of about
200,000 or so, so it's a small city. So ... yeah, check it out.

adapted from: Lost Outback Podcast: Cities of Oz, http://www.lostoutback.com/post/lob021-cities-of-oz/

Ende des Hörverstehenstests

Allgemeiner Hinweis: Die Aussage F: *street markets* bleibt übrig.

1. Melbourne – **G:** cultural life in a big city.
   Hinweis: "So Melbourne is still quite a big city and ... it's not as crowded as Sydney and ... it's more cultural. It's got more of a cultural identity as, as a city." (Z. 33 ff.)

2. Brisbane – **B:** a city centre by a river.
   Hinweis: "... it's a river city. It's got this river that goes right through the centre of the city." (Z. 43 f.)

3. Adelaide – **A:** a place near the dry outback.
   Hinweis: "Actually it's right on the doorstep of the desert." (Z. 47)

4. Perth – **C:** beautiful nature nearby.
   Hinweis: "... it's got a lot of stuff around it to go see as far as natural environment"; "You can go out into the desert and you can go down along the coast to the beaches. Lots of stuff to see."; "It is famous for its beaches ..." (Z. 63 ff.)

5. Darwin – **E:** dangerous wildlife.
   Hinweis: "... it really is kind of crocodiles and snakes and ..."; "Yeah, it's Australia's jungle city." (Z. 75 ff.)

Zweiter Prüfungsteil: Wortschatz – Leseverstehen – Schreiben

Aufgabe 4 – *Lost in the Australian bush*

4.1 Wortschatz

1. a) learn
2. important/difficult
3. b) message.
4. cope/deal/live
5. c) on
6. kill/catch/hunt
7. live/survive
8. b) scared
9. know/realise
10. c) Besides

11. desperate/tired/lonely/bad
12. what (things)
13. d) risky

4.2 Leseverstehen

1. b) ... an unexpected surprise.
   Hinweis: "Jamie Neale, 18, from London, was miraculously found alive and well by two Australian walkers." (Z. 4 f.)

2. c) ... a well-known tourist attraction.
   Hinweis: "Jamie went for a walk in the Blue Mountains, about two hours inland from Sydney, a popular place for tourists who like adventures, ..." (Z. 8 f.)

3. d) ... was able to find food.
   Hinweis: "He survived because he ate seeds, leaves and lettuce-like plants." (Z. 16)

4. b) ... he was found by chance.
   Hinweis: "But then, two Aussie bushwalkers luckily stumbled upon the teenager yesterday." (Z. 29 f.)

5. a) ... received a message.
   Hinweis: "A text message was sent to Jamie's father." (Z. 33)

6. d) ... wear a special watch.
   Hinweis: "If he goes travelling again, we will get one of those watches with a GPS ..." (Z. 43)

4.3 Schreiben

Hinweis: In den Schreibaufgaben werden dir in dieser Prüfung keine Vorgaben zur Länge deiner Texte gemacht. Achte jedoch darauf, dass du in deinen Texten alle Aspekte der Aufgabenstellungen berücksichtigst und strukturiere deine Texte sinnvoll. Nimm dir am Ende die Zeit, alles noch einmal aufmerksam durchzulesen.
Aufgaben 1 und 2 beziehen sich direkt auf den Lesetext. Lies dir also zuerst die Aufgabenstellung genau durch, damit du weißt, nach welchen Informationen du im Text suchen musst. Dann lies den Text ein weiteres Mal durch und markiere die relevanten Textstellen farbig. So kannst du sicherstellen, dass du keine wichtigen Details übersiehst.

1. Jamie's strategy to survive in the bush was as follows. When his bottle of water was empty, he drank rainwater from leaves and after he had eaten his dried fruits, he ate seeds, leaves and plants which were like lettuce. He even ate earthworms.

   During the night he wore his jacket to keep warm and even slept under a log once.

   When he noticed the helicopters in the air above him, he tried to be heard by shouting, but they couldn't hear him. He then tried to be seen more easily by walking up to higher ground. This strategy was not successful either.

   400 people looked for him with helicopters and dogs. Policemen, fire brigade officers, park rangers, emergency service volunteers and even his father joined the search operation.

   However, in the end it was two Australian bushwalkers who found him. One of them was even able to give him medical help. *(152 words)*

2. This is what Jamie's parents think and feel before the rescue. Jamie's father Richard is probably worried and flies out to help in the search operation. However, he believes in the success of it the whole time. Jamie's mother Jean never gives up hope either. She is convinced that Jamie will be rescued and says so to all their family and friends. This optimistic attitude keeps everybody strong.

   After the rescue his father is happy when he sees his son in hospital. He can't believe that his son walked into the bush without a mobile phone. When Mr. Neale receives the phone message he is very excited. He is at a hotel with strangers around him and shouts that his son is alive. Mother and father are relieved and insist that next time their son must wear a special watch with a GPS.

   Jamie's parents love him and it is a terrible thing for parents when their child is missing. But when you love someone you feel responsible for them and you never give up hope. *176 words*

3. a) Jamie went on an adventure trip in the Blue Mountains on his own. It is not easy to answer the question if you should go on such a trip alone.

   On the one hand, young people like to live an adventure, because they want the excitement of new experiences. Those things make them feel stronger. As many young people adore heroes, they want to become heroes themselves. Going on such an adventure trip in Australia or in another adventurous place allows them to experience freedom. In addition, they learn a lot about themselves and get to know a new and very different country.

   On the other hand, adventure trips include risks, so very good preparation is a must. However, when you go on such an adventure trip you cannot avoid every risk. There may be things you have never heard of. When you risk too much, you might get into trouble and even risk other people's lives, for example when you go hiking in remote areas or get close to dangerous or poisonous animals. Apart from that, if you get lost, you might have to pay for your rescue operation.

In my opinion adventure trips are a very special experience in life. It is important for such a trip that you be well-prepared and well-informed. Then it will be a positive experience you will never forget.   *226 words*

b) **12 days scared in the Australian bush**
   Tips on how to avoid risks

   I want to tell you what I experienced during my adventure trip in Australia. An exciting trip soon became a nightmare, because I lost my way in the Blue Mountains and wasn't rescued until twelve days later. I must admit that I hadn't planned the trip well enough. If you want to go on an adventure trip yourself, you should definitely be better prepared. Here are some tips for you.

   My first tip is to have a mobile phone with you, so that you can contact people if necessary. Remember to charge your mobile the night before the trip and take extra batteries with you. There is no electricity in the desert!

   After two days I ran out of food and water. I drank rainwater and even had to eat earthworms. Therefore, my second tip is that you take enough food and water with you for at least several days.

   During the night it became very cold in the desert. My third tip is to have warm clothes and a blanket or sleeping-bag with you.

   During the twelve days alone in the desert I saw and heard the rescue helicopters, but they couldn't see or hear me. My fourth tip is that you have something with you to be seen or heard, like signal rockets or simply a small mirror.

   After I was found, my parents said that it would have been helpful if I had had a watch with a GPS. Therefore, my fifth tip is to buy one before you go on such a trip.

   I was lucky that two Australian bushwalkers found me. I suppose everything would have been easier if I hadn't been on my own. Thus, my last tip is never to go alone on such a trip.

   I will never forget that adventure trip, and I won't make the same mistakes again. It is very important to be well-prepared and well-informed. I hope my tips will help you. Then your trip will be a very special experience for you.   *335 words*

Erster Prüfungsteil: Hörverstehen

1   Selektives Verstehen: *Teen Inc. – What's up at Husky High?*

The Teen Inc. Volunteer Team of Husky High is going to give an overview of their school activities. You are going to hear their announcements for the following weeks.

- *First read the example (0) and the notices (1–5).*
- *Then listen to the announcements.*
- *Complete the notices while you are listening.*
- *At the end you will hear the announcements again.*
- *Now read the example (0) and the notices (1–5). You have 60 seconds to do this.*

Now listen to the announcements and complete the notices.

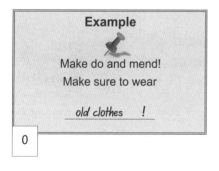

Example

Make do and mend!
Make sure to wear

old clothes !

0

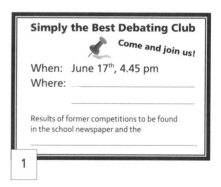

Simply the Best Debating Club

Come and join us!

When: June 17ᵗʰ, 4.45 pm
Where: _____

Results of former competitions to be found in the school newspaper and the
_____ .

1

School T-Shirt Design Contest:

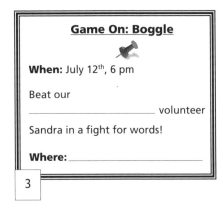

Be a fashion designer!

Win a _____
gift voucher!

Hand in your ideas to Mary Gates
by_____

at the latest!

2

Game On: Boggle

When: July 12th, 6 pm

Beat our

_____ volunteer

Sandra in a fight for words!

Where:_____

3

Nights Owls Radio

Listen to our special guest talk about
his work as a

_____ !

He'll help raise money for Husky High's

_____ in Ruanda!

Interested?

4

Seniors meet Freshmen

Survive at Husky High thanks to

first hand _____

from KaeBee and Kent!

Where: _____

When: Monday–Friday, 9 am–4 pm

5

2 Detailliertes Verstehen: *This is America!*

QES Radio runs a program called "This is America!"
which is a well-known broadcast in and outside the US.
You are going to hear their latest program.

- *First read the tasks (1–10).*
- *Then listen to the program,*
- *Tick the correct box for each task while you are listening.*
- *Tick only **one** box for each task.*
- *At the end you will hear the program again.*
- *Now read the tasks (1–10). You have 2 minutes to do this.*

Now listen to the program and tick the correct box for each task.

1. "This is America!" …
   a) ☐ runs once a week.
   b) ☐ presents today's life stories.
   c) ☐ discusses politics.

2. In the Wild West mail was usually transported …
   a) ☐ by ship.
   b) ☐ by stagecoach.
   c) ☐ on horses.

3. Then Bob talks about …
   a) ☐ advantages of modern communication.
   b) ☐ past communication standards.
   c) ☐ today's communication problems.

4. Delivering mail via land …
   a) ☐ took over 25 days.
   b) ☐ was a governmental project.
   c) ☐ was John Butterfield's idea.

5. John Butterfield planned a route that …
   a) ☐ went right through the Rockies.
   b) ☐ could only be traveled in summer.
   c) ☐ was suitable for the stagecoaches.

6. Safety problems were …
   a) ☐ not talked about by the company.
   b) ☐ seen throughout the whole trip.
   c) ☐ taken care of by a two-man team.

7. The passengers …
   a) ☐ could not lie down.
   b) ☐ had to look after themselves.
   c) ☐ paid a small amount of money.

8. The coaches had to reach San Francisco …
   a) ☐ with only 40 stops.
   b) ☐ two times a day.
   c) ☐ within a time limit.

9. Today …
   a) ☐ there is nothing left of the old stations.
   b) ☐ you can visit some original buildings.
   c) ☐ short tours by stagecoach are offered.

10. Thinking about it again, Bob …
    a) ☐ can easily see past problems.
    b) ☐ is very impressed.
    c) ☐ wants a second show on the topic.

3 Globales Verstehen: *Teen drivers*

You are going to hear a radio program. Sophia Skalbania is asking different people what cars mean to them.
You are going to hear what Steve, Laura, Kevin, Linda, Mr Miller and Mrs Spark have to say.

- *First read the statements (A–G) and look at the list of speakers (0–5).*
- *Then listen to the program.*
- *Choose the correct statement for each speaker and write the letters in the correct boxes.*
- *There is an **example** at the **beginning (0)**.*
- *There is one more statement than you need.*
- *At the end you will hear the program again.*
- *Now read the statements (A–G). You have 30 seconds to do this.*

Now listen to the program and choose the correct statement for each speaker.

Statements		Speakers	Answers
A	Driving your own car is often more than necessary.	0 – Steve (Example)	D
B	Using the bus to get from A to B can be annoying.	1 – Laura	
C	A good public transport system should always be used.	2 – Kevin	
D	**You can't do without a car in the US.**	3 – Linda	
E	Going by car is much cooler than travelling green.	4 – Mr Miller	
F	Having a car means personal freedom.	5 – Mrs Spark	
G	Teenagers depend on their parents to drive them around for too long.		

4 *Don't let your future surprise you!*

4.1 Wortschatz

This text (sentences 1–13) gives some advice to young people who would like to start working after leaving school.

> • *Sentences 1, 3, 5, 10, 12, 13: Tick the correct box (there is only one correct answer).*
> • *Sentences 2, 4, 6, 7, 8, 9, 11: Fill in suitable words.*

1. If you are interested in working with people you need …
   a) ☐ detailed   b) ☐ serious
   c) ☐ social   d) ☐ qualified
   skills.

2. Especially bigger companies use _____ in newspapers to find new employees.

3. Many teenagers have already applied …
   a) ☐ at   b) ☐ by
   c) ☐ for   d) ☐ in
   jobs and know how to do it correctly.

4. Most of the young people know that they have to include their _____ _____ which lists details about their lives.

5. Do not forget to …
   a) ☐ answer   b) ☐ describe
   c) ☐ make   d) ☐ sign
   your letter of application.

6. Before you actually go to a job _____ you should find out details about the company or organisation that has invited you.

7. Some companies have offices in other European countries. This makes them interesting for candidates who would like to work _____.

8. In addition to their own language, international companies often expect their future employees to speak at least two _____ languages fluently.

9. Getting some work _____ will help you to find out about your personal likes and dislikes.

10. It also helps you to …
a) ☐ find   b) ☐ have
c) ☐ make   d) ☐ see
a decision about your future employment.

11. If you need some _____ you can also go to your local job centre.

12. Once you've started your new job you should …
a) ☐ remember   b) ☐ remind
c) ☐ think   d) ☐ find
what you have learned about proper behaviour, of course.

13. a) ☐ Although   b) ☐ Despite
c) ☐ Still   d) ☐ Even
you might sometimes be disappointed, do not give up.

4.2 Leseverstehen

The following text is about an initiative at a school to prepare students for the world of work.

- *First read the text.*
- *Then do the tasks (1–6).*

Don't let your future surprise you!
Students of Centennial High discover the world of work.
by Sarah Witherspoon, 17

1 "When I was your age, I was already working!" – is what my grandpa keeps telling me all the time. Or "You must make up your mind what to do after school!" is my parents' almost daily reminder. But actually they're quite right!

Work experience really is an issue in nearly all schools. Rightly so?

5 Take for instance Centennial High School in Roswell. They run a special career and education program in order to prepare their students for life after school. "Over Years 10 and 11 they spend 50 days gaining[1] experience with an employer," explains Geoffrey Hatcher, principal of Centennial High. "And it's part of our policy that our students spend 20 of these 50 days in doing some kind
10 of social work."

The students can choose between working full-time for one to three weeks and spending one day per week in the workplace over a number of months. So the school's motto "Don't let your future surprise you!" really seems to be true.

There are teachers who express their concern that students might get behind
15 in classes. They think that especially for students with bad marks in several

school subjects and little interest in learning there is really no point in doing work experience.

Yet, there are more important things than the lessons students miss while they are working. The majority of teachers feel that it is necessary to give young
20 people the opportunity to gain good knowledge about the world of work.

"Work experience is the one chance when you get to discover a job you want to do in the future, with the back-up of the school," says Ashley Tumble Tots, 15.

Centennial High coordinator Sue Brendan makes it clear that students need to find out what they want in life. "During their placements, our students get the
25 once-in-a-lifetime chance to enter places that are normally not open to them. Of course there are also times when they will want to run away ... But don't! It's worth it." And this is exactly what happened to poor Nayyab, 17, on his first day at work. He declares: "It was horrible at first ... I didn't know what to say or do. But after some time, you realize a lot about the type of person you are."

30 "For our school it is also important to break up stereotypes of traditional boys' or girls' jobs," Mrs Brendan stresses. "So we cannot provide everyone with his or her dream job, of course." That was Brian's problem, too. He has always been interested in computers and would have liked to work in the telecommunication business. But his school sent him to the local hospital where he had to
35 work as a male nurse. "It was a terrible experience for me," Brian says, "I could not stand all the suffering I saw every day because it made me feel so helpless most of the time. But I realized what a great job nurses do every day, so I do have much more respect for them now."

Lewis, 16, who worked at the local newspaper agency
40 for two weeks, states that his interest in making a career in journalism has grown. Just like Lucy, 16, who worked at a veterinary surgeon's. She says: "Work experience – throw yourself right into it! You've nothing to lose but lots to gain."

45 So work experience seems to be a rather controversial issue[2]. How do you feel about all this ... Write and tell us about your experience for our e-zine's[3] next edition.

Text © Centennial High School (Originaltext zu Prüfungszwecken verändert)
Foto © Josef Muellek/Dreamstime.com

Annotations
1 to gain – to get
2 controversial issue – a heavily debated topic
3 e-zine – an online magazine

1. At Centennial High students have to …
   a) ☐ do their work experience in grades 10 and 11.
   b) ☐ spend 50 days doing social work.
   c) ☐ work full-time for three weeks.
   d) ☐ work one day per week over two years.

2. Most teachers at Centennial High …
   a) ☐ are worried about some pupils' school performance.
   b) ☐ think school is more important than work experience.
   c) ☐ do not want their pupils to miss lessons.
   d) ☐ support the program run by their school.

3. Sue Brendan points out that work experience …
   a) ☐ can be done only once.
   b) ☐ is not open to everybody.
   c) ☐ gives the pupils access to special jobs.
   d) ☐ is not always worth it.

4. Nayyab states that work experience …
   a) ☐ was quite easy right from the start.
   b) ☐ made him feel terrible all the time.
   c) ☐ was a great time for him.
   d) ☐ helped him to find out about himself.

5. Brian reports that he …
   a) ☐ has changed his attitude towards nurses.
   b) ☐ had a typical "boy job".
   c) ☐ had problems in finding a job.
   d) ☐ worked in telecommunications.

6. According to Lucy work experience …
   a) ☐ made her find her future job.
   b) ☐ is something you should not miss.
   c) ☐ was a waste of time.
   d) ☐ was too tiring.

4.3 Schreiben

> - *Read the tasks carefully.*
> - *Write complete sentences and use connectives to link your ideas.*
> - *Make sure to write about **all** the aspects presented in each task.*

1. **Describe** Centennial High's work experience program and **point out** the intention behind it.

2. **Explain** what the teachers and students of Centennial High think about the school's work experience programs.

3. You have a choice here. Choose **one** of the following tasks:

   a) All students at Centennial High have to do some extra social work as part of their work experience. Do you think German pupils should have to do the same?
   Find **arguments for and against** such work experience and state your **personal opinion**.

   or

   b) At the end of the article readers are invited to write about their work experiences. Write an **email** for the e-zine's next edition. Explain what your school does to prepare you for your future working life. Also write about your personal work experience and if you think it was helpful. Give reasons.

Erster Prüfungsteil: Hörverstehen

Mittlerer Schulabschluss – Haupttermin

Wichtige Hinweise: Alle Texte, die du im Folgenden hörst, werden zweimal vorgespielt. Vor dem ersten Hören hast du Zeit, dich mit den Aufgaben vertraut zu machen. Der Hörverstehenstest besteht aus drei Teilen.

1 Selektives Verstehen: *Teen Inc. – What's up at Husky High?*

The Teen Inc. Volunteer Team of Husky High is going to give an overview of their school activities. You are going to hear their announcements for the following weeks. First read the example (0) and the notices 1 to 5. Then listen to the announcements. Complete the notices while you are listening. At the end you will hear the announcements again.

Now read the example (0) and the notices 1 to 5. You have 60 seconds to do this. (60 seconds' break)

Now listen to the announcements and complete the notices.

1 Hey everyone, today is June 16th. Our *Teen Incorporated* volunteer team is glad to inform you about what will be going on in school in the following weeks.

0
Make do and mend – Tonight we're redecorating our Cosy Corner down in the
5 basement. The walls and chairs need a new coat of paint. So, bring along your brush and make sure to wear old clothes! All ages welcome. Beginning at 6 p.m. sharp. Don't be late and miss all the fun!

1
Simply the Best Debating Club – Needless to say, I guess, but another week's
10 over and our Simply the Best Debating Club meets for discussion at 4.45 p.m., however, not in our usual room E28 on the second floor but outside next to the school canteen. On the agenda are the preparations for the upcoming competition on July 21st. By the way, the results of the last few competitions will be published as usual in the next edition of our school newspaper as well as in our
15 newsletter. So, come and join us and see for yourselves, tomorrow, June 17th.

2

School t-shirt design contest – Always dreamt of being a fashion designer? Design a school t-shirt for all our students yourself and win a $ 50 gift voucher to your local fashion shop. Take any picture that has to do with our school and ma-nipulate it on your computer or design it yourself.

Have the honour of seeing your picture on the 500 t-shirts sold at this year's charity bazaar. So, hand in your ideas to Mary Gates, no later than June 5th. Questions? Please call 206.543.4905.

3

Game On: Boggle – Ever tried Boggle? If not, it's time for you to find out! Sign up for Thursday's contest and participate in the absolutely exciting and hair-rais-ing Game On: Boggle. July 12th at 6 p.m. Meet our German volunteer Sandra and do your best to beat her in a tough fight for words. Be the one who creates the longest word out of the letters given. This time it's even trickier than usual! To test your foreign language skills you're supposed to come up with words in German! Interested? Just join the fun in the assembly hall!

4

Night Owls Radio – Come and join us for our Night Owls Radio recording on Thursday, June 24th between 6.15 and 7 p.m. Thanks to a great deal of effort from our dear teacher Mr. Spalding, we're now happy to announce that we've managed to invite Chris de Lea to the show. Chris will tell us all about his huge experience as a first aid nurse on the African continent. Listen to his fascinating stories of how he and his team solve their daily problems on the world's second largest continent. He'll help us raise money for our twin school in Ruanda. For this Night Owls Radio broadcast tune in on Friday between 10.15 and 11 p.m.

5

Seniors meet freshmen – Congratulations on your decision to attend Husky High! All next year's newcomers, come and meet your future tutors who'll give you first-hand information and tell you anything you need to know to survive the first couple of weeks at your new school. Our seniors KaeBee and Kent will help you get familiar with your new school. If you have any more questions, please check our FAQ or contact us. You'll find us in building C on the first floor. Our tutors' bureau is usually open from Monday to Friday between 9 a.m. and 4 p.m. Hope to see you soon!

That's it for this week. Thanks so much for listening and see you all later!

Now listen to the announcements again and check your answers.

1. Where: **outside/next to the school canteen**
   Results of former competitions to be found in the school newspaper and the **newsletter**.
   ✦ Hinweis: "… our Simply the Best Debating Club meets for discussion … outside next to the school canteen." (Z. 10–12);
   "… the results of the last few competitions will be published … in our news-letter." (Z. 13–15)

2. Win a **$ 50** gift voucher!
   Hand in your ideas to Mary Gates by **5th June/June 5th** at the latest!
   ✦ Hinweis: "Design a school t-shirt for all our students yourself and win a $ 50 gift voucher …" (Z. 18);
   "So, hand in your ideas to Mary Gates, no later than June 5th." (Z. 22)

3. Beat our **German** volunteer Sandra in a fight for words!
   Where: **assembly hall**
   ✦ Hinweis: "Meet our German volunteer Sandra and do your best to beat her in a tough fight for words. (Z. 27/28);
   "Just join the fun in the assembly hall!" (Z. 31)

4. Listen to our special guest talk about his work as a **first aid nurse**.
   He'll help raise money for Husky High's **twin school** in Ruanda!
   ✦ Hinweis: "Chris will tell us all about his huge experience as a first aid nurse on the African continent." (Z. 36/37);
   "He'll help us raise money for our twin school in Ruanda." (Z. 39)

5. Survive at Husky High thanks to first hand **information** from KaeBee and Kent!
   Where: **building C/1st floor/first floor**
   ✦ Hinweis: "… come and meet your future tutors who'll give you first-hand information …" (Z. 43/44);
   "You'll find us in building C on the first floor." (Z. 47)

2 Detailliertes Verstehen: *This is America!*

> *QES Radio runs a program called "This is America!" which is a well-known broadcast in and outside the US. You are going to hear their latest program.*
>
> *First read the tasks 1–10. Then listen to the program. Tick the correct box for each task while you are listening. Tick only one box for each task. At the end you will hear the program again. Now read the tasks 1–10. You have two minutes to do this. (2 minutes' break)*
>
> *Now listen to the program and tick the correct box for each task.*

1   BOB: Welcome to *This is America,* our weekly program on facts and great stories from the past about life in the US outside the political fields. I'm Bob Doughty. With me today is Barbara Klein, director of Guadalupe Mountains National Park in West Texas. Welcome to our show, Barbara. In this week's
5   program we're going to talk about mailing.

    BARBARA: Hi everybody. Yes, but not e-mailing as many of you might think ... It's about real letters that were carried to the American West.

    BOB: So we're being taken back to the times of the Wild West?

    BARBARA: Yes, that's right. In those days the quickest way to travel across the
10   western United States was in a stagecoach, a large wagon pulled by horses.

    BOB: What about the mail? You haven't talked about the mail yet.

    BARBARA: Mail was usually carried west on ships that sailed around the bottom of South America and then north to California. That could take several months.

15   BOB: Ugh, that sounds unbelievable compared to modern communication standards. Today we're used to communicating worldwide within seconds. You can even see the person you want to tell something. But that's off the topic. So, what really happened in those days?

    BARBARA: Well, in 1857, the government offered to help any company that
20   wanted to make it possible to send mail all the way across the US by land. A man named John Butterfield accepted this offer. He developed plans for a company that would carry the mail – and passengers, too, from Saint Louis to San Francisco in twenty-five days or less.

    BOB: What about the route? Wasn't it difficult to travel such a long distance at
25   the time?

    BARBARA: Oh, yes, it really was. It was impossible to travel straight through because of the Rocky Mountains and the deep snow that fell in winter. The route they had to take was about 4,500 kilometers. So John Butterfield had to plan the way the stagecoach would travel and built two hundred small sta-

30 tions for the workers and animals along the route at which the horses could
be changed.

BOB: How about safety problems?

BARBARA: Well, of course there were problems. The company even warned passengers about possible risks because the coaches passed through dangerous
35 areas. Some Indians did not want anyone to get near to their settlements. So
two-man teams were responsible for the safety of the mail, the passengers
and the stagecoach.

BOB: So the tour was quite an adventure, wasn't it? ... And not very comfort-
able ...

40 BARBARA: No, not really. The passengers had to sleep on the seats inside, which
could be folded down to make beds, ... or worse, even on the bags of mail.
And it wasn't cheap at all! The cost would be 150 dollars to travel from
Saint Louis to San Francisco and they even had to provide for their own
food.

45 BOB: Does that mean that they travelled non-stop?

BARBARA: The Butterfield Overland Mail stagecoach needed to travel as fast as
possible and it had to keep moving to reach San Francisco in 25 days. So the
coaches only stopped for 40 minutes, two times a day.

BOB: Are there any remains of the stations along the former route that can be
50 visited by tourists today?

BARBARA: Yes, actually there are. Today, the buildings are no longer there, but
tourists can still see the outlines of where they stood, and some of the old
bricks. Besides there are stagecoach rides for visitors.

BOB: Thank you very much for telling us all about this fascinating part of our
55 nation's history, Barbara. People at the time had to be geniuses to overcome
all those troubles, hard for us to imagine today. Perhaps we should run another broadcast on this topic. Haha ... no, just kidding. But, and I feel our
listeners will agree with me there, I still prefer today's ways of communication.

60 Next week on our program, ...

Now listen to the program again and check your answers

1. a) runs once a week.
   Hinweis: "*Welcome to* This is America, *our weekly program on facts and
   great stories ...*" (*Z. 1*)

2. a) by ship.
   Hinweis: "*Mail was usually carried west on ships that sailed around the
   bottom of South America and then north to California.*" (*Z. 12/13*)

2011-14

3. a) advantages of modern communication.

   ✒ *Hinweis: "... that sounds unbelievable compared to modern communication standards. Today we're used to communicating worldwide within seconds ..." (Z. 15/16)*

4. b) was a governmental project.

   ✒ *Hinweis: "... the government offered to help any company that wanted to make it possible to send mail all the way across the US by land." (Z. 19/20)*

5. c) was suitable for the stagecoaches.

   ✒ *Hinweis: "So John Butterfield had to plan the way the stagecoach would travel and built two hundred small stations for the workers and animals along the route ..." (Z. 28–30)*

6. c) taken care of by a two-man team.

   ✒ *Hinweis: "... So two-man teams were responsible for the safety of the mail, the passengers and the stagecoach." (Z. 35–37)*

7. b) had to look after themselves.

   ✒ *Hinweis: "... they even had to provide for their own food." (Z. 43/44)*

8. c) within a time limit.

   ✒ *Hinweis: "The Butterfield Overland Mail stagecoach needed to travel as fast as possible and it had to keep moving to reach San Francisco in 25 days." (Z. 46/47)*

9. c) short tours by stagecoach are offered.

   ✒ *Hinweis: "Besides there are stagecoach rides for visitors." (Z. 53)*

10. b) is very impressed.

    ✒ *Hinweis: "Thank you very much for telling us all about this fascinating part of our nation's history, Barbara. People at the time had to be geniuses to overcome all those troubles, hard for us to imagine today." (Z. 54–56)*

3 Globales Verstehen: *Teen drivers*

> *You are going to hear a radio program. Sophia Skalbania is asking different people what cars mean to them. You are going to hear what Steve, Laura, Kevin, Linda, Mr Miller and Mrs Spark have to say. First read the statements A–G and look at the list of speakers 0–5. Then listen to the program. Choose the correct statement for each speaker and write the letters in the correct boxes. There is an example at the beginning (0). There is one more statement than you need. At the end you will hear the program again. Now read the statements A–G. You have thirty seconds to do this. (30 seconds' break)*
> *Now listen to the program and choose the correct statement for each speaker.*

1 SOPHIA: Hi, I'm Sophia Skalbania for Weekday High. Today I'm talking to new and experienced drivers about what their autos mean to them. Hello to all of you!

ALL: Hey./Hi there./Hi./Hello.

5 SOPHIA: Steve, you start.

STEVE: Yeah, thanks. But first, I've a riddle for you. What goes on three wheels in the morning, on four wheels at noon and on two wheels in the evening? The answer: man. He rides a tricycle as a child, drives a car as an adult and uses a walker in old age. Clever, I know, hahaha … !

10 But the truth is that in America we are likely to be on four wheels our whole life! We like to say that society is greening up, but we are still pretty much a car culture. We are such a huge country. We are a nation on wheels – no doubt about that.

SOPHIA: Clear statement, Steve. So Laura, do you agree?

15 LAURA: Well, erm … I know I should prefer the bus and I know it's better for the environment. So, erm … I feel it's necessary to take the bus more often than driving, but driving is a lot quicker. Apart from that it's great fun to sit in your own car. My friends drive for the most part and they also think they're really trendy when they drive. I'm sure that has affected me. So I got

20 my licence pretty soon after my 16th birthday and …

KEVIN: Sorry to interrupt you. Laura, but …

SOPHIA: Sure, go ahead, Kevin.

KEVIN: Well, I think it's not a question of being trendy. I used to take the bus and it just took a really long time even though it was inexpensive. And

25 sometimes a bus doesn't exactly take you to where you need to go. You just get off in the middle of nowhere and you have to walk a couple of blocks or even a mile. I mean, I'm not saying I shouldn't walk but I'm saying using public transport often takes too long.

SOPHIA: Well, I guess everyone can tell stories like these … So what about you

30 guys? Linda …?

LINDA: Erm … I think a bit like both of you and I do share your point, Kevin. But why are cars so popular especially with young people? Everybody who can afford it gets himself a car. Me too! I guess it's because I wanted to be independent. I was so excited to get a car. When you have your own car, you

35 can decide when to come and go. You know, I don't like to rely on my parents or friends to get me where I need to be.

SOPHIA: Mr Miller, you are nodding as if you agree …

MR MILLER: … Absolutely. I totally agree with you, Linda. See, with my two daughters, transport mainly means me driving my kids. Here in England

40 teenagers have to wait until they're 17. It's just unfair because in the States young people can drive before they turn 17. I often drive my daughters to the

next local town, because public transport services in our little village are useless. I can't wait till they finally get their driving licence.

SOPHIA: I have to admit, I'm a bit surprised at the adult perspective. Mrs Spark, you've got a kid, too. What's your opinion?

MRS SPARK: I do see your point there, Mr Miller. But on the other hand individual driving is pure extravagance. And it's a general question of responsibility towards future generations.

My husband and I, we persuade our son to take the bus as much as we can. Where we live we've got such a great transport system. It's an excellent network that takes you anywhere you like. I really think it's unnecessary for most teens to drive to high school. If you're close to the bus route, you know, there just really isn't much point in it.

KEVIN: I don't quite get it. What do you mean? Your last point …

Now listen to the program again and check your answers.

Ende des Hörverstehenstests.

🖋 **Allgemeiner Hinweis:** *Die Aussage A ("Driving your own car is often more than necessary.") bleibt übrig.*

1. Laura – **E:** Going by car is much cooler than travelling green.
   🖋 *Hinweis: "Well, erm … I know I should prefer the bus and I know it's better for the environment … My friends drive for the most part and they also think they're really trendy when they drive. I'm sure that has affected me." (Z. 15–19)*

2. Kevin – **B:** Using the bus to get from A to B can be annoying.
   🖋 *Hinweis: "I used to take the bus and it just took a really long time … And sometimes a bus doesn't exactly take you to where you need to go. You just get off in the middle of nowhere … I'm not saying I shouldn't walk but I'm saying using public transport often takes too long." (Z. 23–28)*

3. Linda – **F:** Having a car means personal freedom.
   🖋 *Hinweis: "… I wanted to be independent … When you have your own car, you can decide when to come and go." (Z. 33–35)*

4. Mr Miller – **G:** Teenagers depend on their parents to drive them around for too long.

   Hinweis: *"... Here in England teenagers have to wait until they're 17. It's just unfair because in the States young people can drive before they turn 17 ... I can't wait till they finally get their driving licence." (Z. 39–43)*

5. Mrs Spark – **C:** A good public transport system should always be used.

   Hinweis: *"... Where we live we've got such a great transport system. It's an excellent network that takes you anywhere you like. I really think it's unnecessary for most teens to drive to high school. If you're close to the bus route, you know, there just really isn't much point in it." (Z. 50–53)*

Zweiter Prüfungsteil: Wortschatz – Leseverstehen – Schreiben

4 *Don't let your future surprise you!*

4.1 Wortschatz

1. c) social

2. ads/adverts/advertisements

3. c) for

4. CV/Curriculum Vitae

5. d) sign

6. interview

7. abroad/in a foreign country

8. foreign/other

9. experience

10. c) make

11. advice/help/information

12. a) remember

13. a) Although

4.2 Leseverstehen

1. a) do their work experience in grades 10 and 11.
    Hinweis: "Over Years 10 and 11 they spend 50 days gaining experience with an employer ..." (Z. 7/8)

2. d) support the program run by their school.
    Hinweis: "The majority of teachers feel that it is necessary to give young people the opportunity to gain good knowledge about the world of work." (Z. 19/20)

3. c) gives the pupils access to special jobs.
    Hinweis: "During their placements, our students get the once-in-a-lifetime chance to enter places that are normally not open to them." (Z. 24/25)

4. d) helped him to find out about himself.
    Hinweis: "But after some time, you realize a lot about the type of person you are." (Z. 29)

5. a) has changed his attitude towards nurses.
    Hinweis: "But I realized what a great job nurses do every day, so I do have much more respect for them now." (Z. 37/38)

6. b) is something you should not miss.
    Hinweis: "Work experience – throw yourself right into it! You've nothing to lose but lots to gain." (Z. 42–44)

4.3 Schreiben

Hinweis: In den Schreibaufgaben werden dir keine Vorgaben zur Länge deiner Texte gemacht. Achte jedoch darauf, dass du in deinen Texten alle Aspekte der Aufgabenstellungen berücksichtigst und strukturiere deine Texte sinnvoll. Nimm dir am Ende die Zeit, alles noch einmal aufmerksam durchzulesen.

Aufgaben 1 und 2 beziehen sich direkt auf den Lesetext. Lies dir also zuerst die Aufgabenstellungen genau durch, damit du weißt, nach welchen Informationen du im Text suchen musst. Dann lies den Text ein weiteres Mal durch und markiere die relevanten Textstellen farbig. So kannst du sicherstellen, dass du keine wichtigen Details übersiehst.

1. *Hinweis:* In deinem Text kannst du Formulierungen aus dem Lesetext übernehmen. Achte aber darauf, dass dein Text insgesamt eine Einheit bildet; es ist nicht ausreichend, Sätze aus dem Text einfach nur aneinanderzureihen. Bemühe dich, die Sätze sinnvoll miteinander zu verbinden und möglichst eigenständige Formulierungen zu verwenden.

Centennial High School in Roswell runs a special career and education program, because they want to prepare their students for life after school. Students in Years 10 and 11 do 50 days of work experience, and they have to work 20 out of these 50 days in the social field. The students can either work full-time for up to three weeks or spend one day per week with an employer for several months. The motto of the program is "Don't let the future surprise you!"

The intention of the program is for students to get to know the world of work and especially the world of social work. The program is a chance for them to discover what they want to do later. Another intention is to break up stereotypes of traditional boys' and girls' jobs.

2. ✎ *Hinweis: Beginne den Text mit einem einleitenden Satz, der die Aufgabenstellung aufnimmt und zusammenfasst.*

There are various opinions on the work experience program at Centennial High, both among the teachers and the students.

Some teachers are worried that students, especially those who have got bad marks in some subjects and who are not interested in studying, might get behind in class. However, most teachers think that the students benefit from the experience and gain valuable knowledge about the working world. As the school's coordinator points out, students must find out what they want to do later in life. With this program they get the opportunity to look into jobs which they normally would not have access to.

The students of Centennial High mainly think positively about the program. One girl says that work experience is the students' chance to learn more about the job they want to do in the future. Another student emphasizes that everyone should make the most of the work placement, because there is 'nothing to lose, but lots to gain'. Other students think that they have learned a lot about themselves as a person or that they have realized how difficult certain jobs are. Consequently, they have now got great respect for people doing these jobs.

However, not all students feel that way. Some of them have a hard time in the beginning of their work placement, because the situation is completely new for them. They feel insecure and would like to run away. In some cases, the entire experience is horrible for the students, but they usually learn something from it anyway.

3. a) All students at Centennial High have to do some extra social work as part of their work experience. The question whether German students should have to do the same cannot be easily answered, as various aspects have to be considered.

On the one hand, students learn a lot about themselves. They also learn that they can do much more than they would have thought possible and become more self-confident as a consequence. They also find out how hard it is to look after old people or work as a nurse, for example. It is likely that students have to do jobs which they would not choose themselves and which they probably will need time to get used to. For many students working in an old people's home or a hospital is not a dream job, but they learn to take responsibility, which will improve their social skills.

On the other hand, some students at that age might not be able to cope with difficult situations, because they are still quite young. They might make mistakes or might not take the job seriously. Consequently, a lot of them could be sent home due to this fact. With this negative experience these students will never think of doing any kind of social work again.

In my opinion, work experience in the social field gives students lots of respect for the work of others. They learn a lot about themselves and skills which they will need in their future lives in all kinds of jobs. All in all, I believe it is a good idea to make social work part of students' work experience.

b) *Hinweis: Hier schreibst du eine E-Mail an das Team der Centennial High, das das Online-Magazin der Schule betreut. Deine Zuschrift wird auf der Homepage veröffentlicht werden. Du solltest also das Datum und eine Anrede wählen, sowie am Ende deinen Namen, deinen Wohnort und dein Alter nennen.*

9th June 2011

Hello,

I am referring to your article "Don't let the future surprise you!", which was about the work experience program of Centennial High in Roswell in the last edition of your online magazine. I am writing to tell you about how my school prepares students for their future working lives, about my personal work experience and how I feel about such programs.

My first experience with the world of work was in Year 8, when we had the 'Girls' and Boys' Day' and I worked at a hairdresser's. At my school students have to do two weeks of work experience both in Years 9 and 10. In Year 9 a job is found for us by the school, but in Year 10 we have to look for a job on our own. One subject at our school is *Arbeitslehre* where we learn about the world of work. Apart from that, we are taught how to write a letter of application, a CV and how to present ourselves in a job interview in our German lessons. In our English lessons we learn how to do all those things in English, and we even have some lessons in business English. Usually, students visit the local job centre at least once together with their class teacher at the end of their school career, so that they know how everything works there and in order to find out where chances are best to get a job.

In Year 9 I worked as a mechanic at a garage, which was very interesting. I liked working there, but the boss of the garage told me that the chances of getting a job in this field after leaving school were rather slim.

In year 10 I worked as a nurse in a hospital. It was hard work, both physically and emotionally, but I liked helping other people and I was told that the chances of getting a job there were much better. Actually, they told me to apply right away, so this work experience was very helpful for me.

To sum up, I would like to say that work experience is very important and helpful for all students who don't want to be surprised by their future.

Peter, 16, Cologne

Erster Prüfungsteil: Hörverstehen – Leseverstehen

1 Hörverstehen Teil 1: *Stan Lee*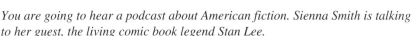

You are going to hear a podcast about American fiction. Sienna Smith is talking to her guest, the living comic book legend Stan Lee.

- *First read the tasks (1–9).*
- *Then listen to the podcast.*
- *Tick the correct box or complete the sentences while you are listening.*
- *Tick only **one** box.*
- *At the end you will hear the podcast again.*
- *Now read the tasks (1–9). You have 90 seconds to do this.*

1. The comic writer is …
   a) ☐ known by many teenagers.
   b) ☐ very old.
   c) ☐ mostly known by his real name.

2. In his childhood, Stan Lee liked reading books about _____
   _____.

3. As a child, Stan Lee …
   a) ☐ played his favourite films.
   b) ☐ was a fan of an actor.
   c) ☐ wanted to become a sheriff.

4. At school, Stan's teachers supported him to _____.

5. Becoming a comic writer was …
   a) ☐ a well-thought-out plan.
   b) ☐ Stan's dream job.
   c) ☐ simply good luck.

6. Stan Lee works best if he is under _____.

7. *Spider-Man* was born …
   a) ☐ when Stan saw a fly one day.
   b) ☐ after *The Fantastic Four* had failed.
   c) ☐ before Stan invented *The Hulk*.

8. Stan thinks superheroes …
   a) ☐ must be muscular.
   b) ☐ are quickly boring.
   c) ☐ should be imperfect.

9. *Spider-Man's* success …
   a) ☐ was a surprise to Stan.
   b) ☐ nearly cost Stan his job.
   c) ☐ was great right away.

2 Hörverstehen Teil 2: *Cooking lessons for students* 💿

Jenna Jones from Radio One Plus X is talking to Mr Ed Balls, the nation's school secretary, who is responsible for the plans to introduce cooking lessons for British students.

- *First read the tasks (1–9).*
- *Then listen to the interview.*
- *Tick the correct box or complete the sentences while you are listening.*
- *Tick only* **one** *box.*
- *At the end you will hear the interview again.*
- *Now read the tasks (1–9). You have 90 seconds to do this.*

1. Three years ago, the government started a programme to _____ school meals.

2. "Cooking lessons" are offered …
   a) ☐ in all British schools.
   b) ☐ from September next year.
   c) ☐ to certain students.

3. Mr Balls thinks schools should help students to become healthy _____
   _____.

4. "Cooking lessons" also teach students to …
   a) ☐ buy food intelligently.
   b) ☐ avoid kitchen accidents.
   c) ☐ use simple ingredients.

5. Mr Balls invites the listeners to send in their suggestions for popular _____
   _____.

6. Emails can be sent to getcooking.consultation@ …
   a) ☐ decf.gse.gov.uk.
   b) ☐ dcsf.gsi.gov.uk.
   c) ☐ dscf.gsa.gov.uk.

7. One dish suggested by a food expert is baked _____ with potatoes.

8. Both students and parents …
   a) ☐ are interested in diet and nutrition.
   b) ☐ support the government's idea.
   c) ☐ like the practical work.

9. Mr Balls regrets that some _____ schools still do not
   have the necessary kitchen equipment.

3   Leseverstehen

Test of courage

1 Perhaps Dilip fell in love with the drum before he was even born.

   Then Mr Robinson moved into the neighbourhood and Dilip began to hear
this amazing music coming out of his open window: It blew his mind[1]. They met
when Mr Robinson almost fell over the boy, sitting on his doorstep, playing in-
5 visible drums on his knees. And that was the start of a beautiful friendship. Mr
Robinson had the feeling he could teach him a thing or two. But one day, Dilip
was approached by one of the gang. "Ravi wants you in. You're one of us now,
you know, Dilip, and to prove it, we have a little task for you. Interested?"

   What they asked of him made Dilip feel sick. It wasn't anything like running
10 across the rails in front of a train, or stealing a car, or putting a brick through a
shop window.

   He'd rather have done any of those things than what they demanded.

   "That old guy you're friendly with." Ravi threw his head in the direction of
Mr Robinson's flat. "He's got money hidden – everyone knows that. He'll have
15 got his pension today. I'm a bit short of cash at the moment, so I want you to get it."

   "I can't do that! He's my friend."

   "You'll do what we say." Ravi looked threatening.

"No! No, I won't!" cried Dilip. "You can't make me do that."

"Oh, can't I?" Ravi came right up to the younger boy, eyeball to eyeball.
20 "Want to try me?", he asked, softly threatening.

"Can we make him do it, Mukki?"

"He'll do it," reassured Mukham. "I'll make sure he does."

"Right then. Get that money. We'll be here waiting for you this time tomorrow. Have it, or else … Gottit?"

25 "Gottit," muttered Dilip weakly.

Mr Robinson was looking tired when he opened the door to Dilip. "Good to see you, mate!" he sighed, welcoming him in.

Dilip felt out of his body. That couldn't be him greeting his friend, coming as a thief and a traitor to betray him – could it? But it was him noticing how slowly
30 Mr Robinson was walking. "You OK?"

"It's been bad today. How's the drumming?"

"Great," answered Dilip in a dead voice.

"Really great. I guess I shouldn't come bothering you day in day out."

"Hey, you were never a bother to me."

35 Mr Robinson's face broke into a smile.

"I like your company, and now you've got your own drum you can practise everything I teach you – and I've still lots more to teach you. Do you want to have a go now?"

"Yeah," said Dilip, his eyes wandering to the mantelpiece[2]. He could see Mr
40 Robinson's pension money hidden as usual behind the clock.

Dilip's voice was so unenthusiastic that Mr Robinson glanced quickly at him with concern. "No one's making you if you don't feel like it." Dilip stood stockstill, his eyes still glued to the money. Was he going to give in? He felt a rush of courage. Turning with a broad smile, he said, "Yeah, please, Mr Robinson. I'd
45 like a bash[3]. We have a gig on Saturday at the Community Centre. It'll be my first big one."

by Jamila Gavin (slightly adapted)

1 it blew his mind – it produced a shocking feeling in Dilip
2 mantelpiece – a shelf above a fireplace
3 bash – try

- *First read the text.*
- *Then do the tasks 1–7.*
- *For tasks 1, 2, 3, 5 and 6 decide if the statements are true or false and tick the correct box. Then finish these sentences. You can quote from the text.*
- *For task 4 fill in the information.*
- *For task 7 tick the correct box. Tick only **one** box for this task.*

1. Mr Robinson awoke Dilip's interest in playing the drums.
   This statement is
   a) ☐ true　　　　　　　　b) ☐ false
   because the text says

   ---

2. Dilip feels miserable when the gang want him to do a job for them.
   This statement is
   a) ☐ true　　　　　　　　b) ☐ false
   because the text says

   ---

3. Ravi thinks that Mr Robinson has some extra money at home.
   This statement is
   a) ☐ true　　　　　　　　b) ☐ false
   because the text says

   ---

4. The gang threaten Dilip and want to force him to steal Mr Robinson's money. How do we know? Give two examples from the text:
   a) _____
   b) _____

5. When Dilip arrives at Mr Robinson's place, everything appears to be normal first.
   This statement is
   a) ☐ true　　　　　　　　b) ☐ false
   because the text says

   ---

6. Mr Robinson likes being visited by Dilip.
   This statement is
   a) ☐ true　　　　　　　　b) ☐ false
   because the text says

   ---

7. By the end of the story, Dilip seems to have changed. How?
   a) ☐ Dilip realizes that he has a choice in what he does.
   b) ☐ Dilip understands that he can't escape group pressure.
   c) ☐ Dilip sees that old people do not understand teenagers.

How can young and old people benefit from each other?

4 Wortschatz: *Many generations under one roof*

Sentences 1–13 form a text about living in a family with parents, grandparents and even more generations.

- *Sentences 2, 4, 5, 8, 10, 12: tick the correct box (there is only **one** correct answer).*
- *Sentences 1, 3, 6, 7, 9, 11, 13: fill in suitable words.*

1. More and more American households _____ three or more generations living together.

2. a) ☐ Also   b) ☐ Although
    c) ☐ Therefore   d) ☐ Despite
    these multigenerational families face a lot of problems, there are also many advantages.

3. It is great for children to get some extra _____ from grandparents.

4. Sometimes, young adults even …
    a) ☐ move   b) ☐ travel
    c) ☐ depart   d) ☐ pass
    back home for different reasons.

5. It is a great help for parents if grandparents take care …
    a) ☐ for   b) ☐ of
    c) ☐ with   d) ☐ on
    their younger children.

6. Older people, on the other hand, feel less _____ when they live around children and grandchildren.

7. The younger generation can _____ their grandparents a lot about modern life.

8. But a multigenerational family needs fixed rules to …
    a) ☐ destroy   b) ☐ create
    c) ☐ miss   d) ☐ avoid
    problems.

9. Each family member must be _____ for a certain job in the house.

10. As everybody needs some privacy, the family should …
    a) ☐ cut   b) ☐ break
    c) ☐ separate   d) ☐ join
    private rooms and family rooms.

11. It is also important to have a special _____ to come together with all the family members.

12. The most important rule is that everybody …
    a) ☐ remembers   b) ☐ reminds
    c) ☐ respects   d) ☐ recalls
    each other's opinion.

13. And remember: each generation plays an important _____ in a multigenerational family.

5   Schreiben

How can young and old people benefit from each other?

1 Electric cars, Tablet PCs, satellite TV, fashion or music styles nobody has ever seen or heard of before – the world we live in is really dynamic – and it is changing daily! Young and old people are confronted with an enormous amount of knowledge and information which quickly becomes outdated[1] again.

5   This is why Melissa Kelly, a secondary school teacher from Prudent High, Wisconsin, organizes a project, in which young and old people get together regularly. According to Mrs. Kelly, "young people possess an ability to learn and pick up information faster and easier. The older generation, however, is not that much interested in fast changes." She claims that many new products and tech-
10 nologies are also of great use for old people and that there is no age limit for learning something new.

       Dan Thorndike, aged 82 and former motor mechanic, proves her right. He took part in her project and explains that "computers were a real mystery" to him. Although he knew that they could be used for emails, social networks and
15 ICQ, he would never trouble himself to learn how to use them.

       Lots of older people are certainly curious about modern ways of communication, but they are often too afraid of not being able to operate them. After making the effort and taking part in Mrs. Kelly's project, Mr. Thorndike is now quite content with himself. Like many other elderly participants he is happy now to be
20 able to carry out useful searches on the Internet or go shopping online from his

home. The fact that he can even see his little granddaughter when phoning her via Internet, is still unbelievable, and yet, very practical for him because she lives thousands of miles away.

Mrs. Kelly explains that one gets something in return when teaching seniors.
25 This is what Julia Jackson (17) from Prudent High School confirms. She spent some part of her free time explaining modern technology to older people. Although she was quite skeptical at the beginning, her first fears soon disappeared and she now enjoys the relaxed atmosphere between the two generations. What's more, she is very proud to be some kind of a teacher!

30 Carl Milton, another student participant in the project, lives with his parents and grandparents. This is why he calls himself an "expert" on generation questions. He thinks that such projects are rather an exchange than a one-way street and points out that the media are not the only link between the two generations. Young people can also bridge the age gap[2] through songs and dances.
35 "Music," so he says, "is a universal language and appreciated[3] by people despite age differences. Music will always have an audience, young and old alike."

Experience shows that there are also other things that young and old people can share.

Mrs. Lockyer from Manchester, for example, says that she would never have
40 thought that her granddaughter could be interested in her collection of handbags. "But as it is," she claims, "old things become fashionable again. And young people need to find their own style. It's a question of identity."

According to Mrs. Kelly traveling can also be valuable for both. Since most young people are active and mobile, they can encourage older people to go out
45 more often. Once a month a group of Mrs. Kelly's students take elderly people to interesting places nearby, so that they can enjoy new sights and sounds.

Every day is always a new day to learn. The older generation can teach aspects of as traditional culture or share valuable life experience. In modern society, however, it is the young who possess updated knowledge and who can be of
50 great help to the old. Mr. Thorndike states that "Thanks to the young generation's know-how, elderly people can keep in touch with the world. But one should not forget that older people also have so much to offer."

1 outdated – *veraltet*
2 gap – *Lücke*
3 to appreciate – *schätzen, würdigen*

1. **Describe** Mrs. Kelly's reasons to get young people and old people together and the fields in which they can benefit from each other.

2. **Explain** the experiences the young and the old people have shared with each other and how these have changed their attitude.

3. You have a choice here. Choose **one** of the following tasks:

   a) "Older people also have so much to offer."
   Discuss the **pros and cons** of this statement from **your** point of view. Explain your opinion and give examples.

   or

   b) On her website, Mrs. Kelly asks young people to present their ideas for projects that bring young and old people together.
   Write an **email** to Mrs. Kelly and present your ideas for a project in your hometown or at your school and give your reasons for wanting to carry it out.

Erster Prüfungsteil: Hörverstehen – Leseverstehen

Mittlerer Schulabschluss – Haupttermin

Wichtige Hinweise: Alle Texte, die du im Folgenden hörst, werden zweimal vor-
gespielt. Vor dem ersten Hören hast du Zeit, dich mit den Aufgaben vertraut zu
machen. Der Hörverstehenstest besteht aus zwei Teilen.

---

1 Hörverstehen Teil 1: *Stan Lee*

You are going to hear a podcast about American fiction. Sienna Smith is talking
to her guest, the living comic book legend Stan Lee. First read the tasks (1–9).
Then listen to the podcast. Tick the correct box or complete the sentences while
*you are listening. Tick only **one** box. At the end you will hear the podcast again.*
Now read the tasks (1–9). You have 90 seconds to do this.

---

1 SIENNA: This is the Chicago fiction podcast. I'm Sienna Smith and I'd like you
to welcome the great Stan Lee, the creator of *Spider-Man, Hulk, The Fan-*
tastic Four and *X-Men.*

STAN LEE: Hi, there!

5 SIENNA: Stan, loads of young people are fascinated by your heroes, but they
hardly know anything about the person who's created them. So, tell us more
about yourself. Erm, your real name is …

STAN LEE: Stanley Martin Lieber, but most people know me as Stan Lee. I was
born in Manhattan, in 1922 … a really long time ago.

10 SIENNA: Do you have any special memories about the time when you were a kid?

STAN LEE: Well, I remember reading those great books about heroes and adventures and of course I remember the movies I went to.

SIENNA: Aha, erm … Who was your favourite superhero, or favourite movie
star?

15 STAN LEE: Mmh .. My favourite movie star, far and away, was Errol Flynn. I
thought that this guy was the greatest, because he always played such heroic
roles. He was either a sheriff, or he was *Robin Hood.* Actually, all my favourite movie stars were always the ones who played heroic roles. And … I always tried to be one of them when I was about 10 years old.

20 SIENNA: Ha – do you have one specific memory when it clicked in your mind
that you wanted to create characters yourself?

STAN LEE: No, not exactly. Err … At school I was always good at writing stories and my teachers always encouraged me to write.

SIENNA: And … erm, who was the first person who believed in your talent?

25 STAN LEE: Well, err, that's an interesting question. I was hired by a comic magazine company to be an assistant. And after a while, they started giving me things to write. In those days comics weren't really highly respected. So I thought I'd stay there for a few months, and then I would try to get into other departments.

30 SIENNA: So, you really didn't plan to write comics?

STAN LEE: Actually, no, not really.

SIENNA: Okay. Erm … How do you plan your work?

STAN LEE: Err … I'm sort of an "under pressure" writer. If somebody says, "Stan, write something," and I have to have it by tomorrow morning, I'll just

35 sit down and write it. I'm better doing a rushed job.

SIENNA: Ha, that's amazing. Do you remember exactly what you were doing when you thought up the idea for *Spider-Man*?

STAN LEE: Actually, yes, I do. I've told this story so often. I'd already done *The Fantastic Four* and *The Hulk,* and they were doing pretty well. One day, I

40 was sitting at my desk when I saw a fly crawling on the floor and I said, "Gee, wouldn't it be cool if I could get a hero who could crawl on walls like an insect?" But then I needed a name for him. I thought about *Insect-* or *Mosquito-Man.* Then I thought up *Spider-Man* and somehow … it … sounded just right.

45 SIENNA: Did you know from the start what this hero should … look like?

STAN LEE: Not exactly, but I really didn't want him to be like these typical muscular superheroes. I wanted him to be an average teenager, who makes mistakes and shows feelings. I think if they are perfect, they become incredibly uninteresting.

50 SIENNA: Could you have ever imagined that *Spider-Man* would become so successful?

STAN LEE: In the early days, when we were doing the books, I never thought that *Spider-Man* would become the world wide icon that he is. I just hoped the books would sell and I'd keep my job.

55 SIENNA: Well, you certainly did. And lucky us. Stan, unfortunately time's up. So, thanks a lot for …

1. b) … very old.
   Hinweis: "I was born in Manhattan, in 1922 … a really long time ago." (Z. 8/9)

2. … heroes/adventures/heroes and adventures

    ✎ *Hinweis:* "*Well, I remember reading those great books about heroes and adventures …*" *(Z. 11/12)*

3. b) … was a fan of an actor.

    ✎ *Hinweis:* "*My favourite movie star, far and away, was Errol Flynn.*" *(Z. 15)*

4. … write.

    ✎ *Hinweis:* "*At school I was always good at writing stories and my teachers always encouraged me to write*" *(Z. 22/23)*

5. c) … simply good luck.

    ✎ *Hinweis:*
    "*SIENNA: So, you didn't really plan to write comics?*
    STAN-LEE: Actually, no, not really." *(Z. 30/31)*

6. … pressure.

    ✎ *Hinweis:* "*Err … I'm sort of an 'under pressure' writer.*" *(Z. 33)*

7. a) … when Stan saw a fly one day.

    ✎ *Hinweis:* "*One day, I was sitting at my desk when I saw a fly crawling on the floor …*" *(Z. 39/40)*

8. c) … should be imperfect.

    ✎ *Hinweis:* "*Not exactly, but I didn't want him to be like these typical muscular superheroes. I wanted him to be an average teenager, who makes mistakes and shows feelings. I think if they are too perfect they become incredibly uninteresting.*" *(Z. 46–49)*

9. a) … was a surprise to Stan.

    ✎ *Hinweis:* "*In the early days, when we were doing the books, I never thought that Spider-Man would become the world wide icon that he is.*" *(Z. 52/53)*

2 Hörverstehen Teil 2: *Cooking lessons for students*

> *Jenna Jones from Radio One Plus X is talking to Mr Ed Balls, the nation's school secretary, who is responsible for the plans to introduce cooking lessons for British students. First read the tasks (1–9). Then listen to the interview. Tick the correct box or complete the sentences while you are listening. Tick only **one** box. At the end you will hear the interview again. Now read the tasks (1–9). You have 90 seconds to do this.*

1 JENNA: This is Radio One Plus X and you are listening to The Morning Talk
with Jenna Jones.
Today we are talking about food and school. As you might already know,
the Government began to improve school dinners three years ago after TV
5 chef Jamie Oliver had fought against the poor quality of food served in
school canteens and cafeterias. But now, a further step is being taken. Like it
or not, you have to take part if your school does. From this September, every
11- to 14-year-old in the 85 per cent of schools offering food technology
classes will be taught practical cookery.
10 Today I would like to welcome Mr Ed Balls, the nation's school secretary.
Good morning Mr Balls, please tell us how you came up with the idea of
establishing compulsory cooking classes.
MR BALLS: Hello, Jenna. Well, teaching kids to cook healthy meals is an important way of how schools can help produce healthy adults.
15 JENNA: Alright. What exactly will be done in these classes?
MR BALLS: Erm, we want to make sure that pupils can master simple, healthy
recipes with fresh ingredients. We also want to include diet and nutrition,
food safety and clever food shopping.
JENNA: OK, sounds interesting, but what recipes are you thinking of?
20 MR BALLS: Of course, we have some suggestions from nutrition experts, but I
want to encourage members of the public to come up with ideas for classic
English dishes and international cuisine. So, if you have any suggestions,
please feel free to email the Government. The email address is
getcooking.consultation@dcsf.gsi.gov.uk. But remember: the dishes must be
25 healthy, simple and the kind of meals that teenagers like to eat.
JENNA: Wow! Sounds like people really can get involved in establishing a national curriculum! But surely our listeners are also interested in the food experts' suggestions that you have mentioned. Can you give us any examples?
MR BALLS: Sure. Fiona Becket, who is a well-known food author, suggests Spa-
30 ghetti Bolognese, risotto, baked chicken with lemony potatoes and as
dessert, fruit with yoghurt.
JENNA: Ha – what about the students and their parents? Do they support the
government's plans?
MR BALLS: Absolutely! Although they both have different reasons, they do, yes.
35 A growing number of parents are aware of questions that have to do with
diet and nutrition. I mean you can easily imagine that parents only want the
best for their kids which is being and staying healthy. In addition to that the
kids like the idea of practical work. It will definitely be an alternative to
other classes.
40 JENNA: But Mr Balls, some schools do not take part in the programme …

MR BALLS: Yes, you're right. The schools that do not offer cooking lessons tend to be all-boys' schools which simply haven't got the equipment yet. But we're already dealing with the problem by installing the necessary kitchen equipment by the end of this year.

45 JENNA: Sounds like tasty times for students! Mr Balls, thank you for answering my questions and thank you for listening today. Tune in tomorrow for another issue of The Morning Talk with Jenna Jones and guests.

1. … improve …
   Hinweis:

2. c) … to certain students.
   Hinweis: "From this September, every 11- to 14-year-old in the 85 per cent of schools offering food technology classes will be taught practical cookery." (Z. 7–9)

3. … adults.
   Hinweis: "Well, teaching kids to cook healthy meals is an important way of how schools can help produce healthy adults."(Z. 13/14)

4. a) … buy food intelligently.
   Hinweis: "We also want to include diet and nutrition, food safety and clever food shopping." (Z. 17/18)

5. … (English) dishes/recipes/(international) cuisine.
   Hinweis: "… but I want to encourage members of the public to come up with ideas for classic English dishes and international cuisine." (Z. 20–22)

6. b) … dcsf.gsi.gov.uk.
   Hinweis: (Z. 23/24)

7. … chicken …
   Hinweis: "Fiona Becket, who is a well-known food author, suggests Spaghetti Bolognese, risotto, baked chicken with lemony potatoes and …" (Z. 29/30)

8. b) … support the government's idea.
   Hinweis:
   "JENNA: Ha – what about the students and their parents? Do they support the government's plans?
   MR BALLS: Absolutely." (Z. 32–34)

9. … (all) boys' …
   Hinweis: "The schools that do not offer cooking lessons tend to be all boys' schools which simply haven't got the equipment yet." (Z. 41/42)

3 Leseverstehen

1. b) false
   "Perhaps Dilip fell in love with the drum before he was even born."
   ✎ Hinweis: (Z. 1)

2. a) true
   "What they asked of him made Dilip feel sick."
   ✎ Hinweis: (Z. 9)

3. a) true
   Ravi says, "He'll have got his pension today."
   ✎ Hinweis: (Z. 14/15)

4. a) Ravi says, "You'll do what we say."
      ✎ Hinweis: (Z. 17)
   b) Mukham says, "I'll make sure he does."
      ✎ Hinweis:(Z. 22)
      Ravi came right up to the younger boy, eyeball to eyeball. "Want to try me?", he asked, softly threatening. / "Have it, or else ... Gottit?"
      ✎ Hinweis: (Z. 19/20, Z. 24)

5. b) false
   "Dilip felt out of his body."
   ✎ Hinweis: (Z. 28)
   "You OK?" "It's been bad today."
   ✎ Hinweis: (Z. 30/31)

6. a) true
   "Hey, you were never a bother to me." Mr Robinson's face broke into a smile. "I like your company ..."
   ✎ Hinweis: (Z. 34–36)

7. a) Dilip realizes that he has a choice in what he does.
   ✎ Hinweis: He felt a rush of courage. Turning with a broad smile, he said, "Yeah, please, Mr Robinson. I'd like a bash." (Z. 43–45)

How can young and old people benefit from each other?

4 Wortschatz: *Many generations under one roof*

1. have / consist of

2. b) Although

3. attention / love / help / money

4. a) move

5. b) of

6. isolated / alone

7. teach / show / tell

8. d) avoid

9. responsible

10. c) seperate

11. room / time / place

12. c) respects

13. role / part

5 Schreiben

Hinweis: In den Schreibaufgaben werden dir keine Vorgaben zur Länge deiner Texte gemacht. Achte jedoch darauf, dass du in deinen Texten alle Aspekte der Aufgabenstellungen berücksichtigst und strukturiere deine Texte sinnvoll. Nimm dir am Ende die Zeit, alles noch einmal aufmerksam durchzulesen und Fehler zu verbessern.
Aufgaben 1 und 2 beziehen sich direkt auf den Lesetext. Lies dir zuerst die Aufgabenstellungen genau durch, damit du weißt, nach welchen Informationen du im Text suchen musst. Dann lies den Text ein weiteres Mal durch und markiere die relevanten Textstellen farbig. So kannst du sicherstellen, dass du keine wichtigen Details übersiehst.

1. *✐ Hinweis: In deinem Text kannst du Formulierungen aus dem Lesetext übernehmen. Achte aber darauf, dass dein Text insgesamt eine Einheit bildet; es ist nicht ausreichend, Sätze aus dem Text einfach nur aneinanderzureihen. Bemühe dich, die Sätze sinnvoll miteinander zu verbinden und möglichst eigenständige Formulierungen zu verwenden.*

The first reason for Mrs. Kelly to get young people and old people together is that the older generation can profit from the younger's knowledge of modern technologies. The second reason is that the young generation gets something in return. They can learn from the old, who have so much to offer.

One field in which both generations can benefit from each other is the use of new products. The young can show the old how to use them. This is particularly true for modern communication technologies. Here, the young can teach the old how to use the computer and especially the internet, how to write an email, to phone via the internet or use social networks.

Other fields where both generations can benefit from each other are music, fashion or travelling. The young can show the old interesting places nearby, so that they can enjoy new sights and sounds.   *150 words*

2. *✐ Hinweis: Hier ist es wichtig, dass du auf die konkreten Erfahrungen von Dan Thorndike, Julia Jackson, Carl Milton und von Frau Lockyer eingehst. Vergiss nicht zu beschreiben, wie sich deren Einstellung geändert hat.*

For Dan Thorndike computers were a real mystery. He knew about the opportunities of the internet but was afraid that he wouldn't understand these new technologies.

After taking part in Mrs. Kelly's project, Dan is very happy. His attitude towards computers has changed. Now he knows how to use them, how to go shopping online, for example, and he can even communicate with his little granddaughter, who lives very far away. Now he can talk and see her via the internet.

Julia Jackson was also very skeptical at the beginning of the project. But that soon changed and now she is very proud that she is a kind of teacher at the age of 17.

Carl Milton is a student who lives with his parents and grandparents. He knows of the advantages of the project. For him such projects are a success because young and old people are able to exchange ideas and experiences. He thinks the modern media is not the only topic. Music and dance can also connect both generations.

Fashion can be another link. Mrs. Lockyer never thought that her grand-daughter could be so interested in her collection of handbags. This was a new experience for her.   *201 words*

3. a) ✦ **Hinweis:** *Bei dieser Aufgabe musst du sowohl Argumente, die der Aussage zustimmen, als auch Argumente, die der Aussage widerspre-chen, nennen. Da du aber aus deiner Perspektive argumentieren darfst, kannst du dir aussuchen, welcher Seite du insgesamt zustimmst. Vergiss nicht, deine Argumentation durch konkrete Beispiele zu stützen.*

The answer to the question whether older people also have so much to offer is not very difficult, because there are so many arguments that underline this fact that young people can only profit from the older generation.

It is often negatively said that older people only speak of the past, but it is important for the young to listen to these stories. They can learn from their experiences in order to avoid making the same mistakes. Additionally, these stories probably help them to understand what they need to do to get a good job or how to complete their education success-fully. It is said that older people do not know much about modern tech-nology, but they know how to live without it. Being part of the modern world of communication can be very stressful for young people. They could learn from the old how to live a calm and peaceful life without mo-dern technologies.

Often people say that old people can be very stubborn. They only give advice, but do not listen to new arguments and ideas. Young people who try to help old people to open their minds to new possibilities make themselves happy, too. They personally feel better, because they helped someone else to feel content. Julia Jackson from Prudent High School is a very good example because she feels proud of what she does.

To come to a conclusion, I think one can say that the statement "Older people also have so much to offer" is absolutely right. But it is important that young people take the initiative to make this statement come true by starting their own projects.   *273 words*

b) *Hinweis:* *Bei dieser Aufgabe musst du eine E-Mail schreiben. Du darfst also die Anrede und die Verabschiedung nicht vergessen. Zu Beginn kannst du dich auf die Aufforderung auf der Internetseite beziehen. Die Aufgabenstellung ist zweiteilig, denn du sollst deine Projektideen präsentieren und zudem begründen, warum diese durchgeführt werden sollten.*

Dear Mrs. Kelly,

I really like your project in which young and old people get together regularly, because they can only benefit from each other. I would like to start a similar project at my school here in Germany. On your website you ask young people to present their ideas for such a project.

Here are mine:In my project there would be regular meetings of young and old people to get to know each other. After that the young and the old could go shopping together. Young people could carry the bags for older people. It would be great if they also helped the older generation in their households. Vice versa the old could help the young with their homework.

Together we could start a project called "Our town in the past and now". Older people could describe what our city looked like many years ago and the young could describe our modern city with all the sights and opportunities. So the older generation would get to know the modern city and the younger generation would learn much more about the history of our town. At the end there would be an exhibition at our school.

With this exhibition probably more older and younger people would become interested in our project and join us or start their own projects. That would be marvellous.

So, what do you think of my ideas? It would be great if you could give me your opinion.

Kind regards,
(your name)   *245 words*

Erster Prüfungsteil: Hörverstehen – Leseverstehen

1   Hörverstehen Teil 1: *Memories of 9/11*

On September 11th, 2001, terrorists directed two planes into the World Trade Center in New York. Lots of people died and the Twin Towers were completely destroyed. Chloe Morton from USspotRadio is reporting live from the 9/11 Tribute Center.

> - *First read the tasks (1–9).*
> - *Then listen to the report.*
> - *Tick the correct box or complete the sentences while you are listening.*
> - *Tick only **one** box.*
> - *At the end you will hear the report again.*
> - *Now read the tasks (1–9). You have 90 seconds to do this.*

1. All the guides of the 9/11 Tribute Center share their stories and
   _____.

2. Instead of the Twin Towers there are two _____.

3. The victims' names are arranged …
   a) ☐ chronologically.
   b) ☐ according to the alphabet.
   c) ☐ next to their colleagues' names.

4. A visitor says that he …
   a) ☐ lives in New York.
   b) ☐ likes the new skyline very much.
   c) ☐ remembers the Twin Towers with sadness.

5. In the new building there will be new offices, as well as _____
   and restaurants under one roof.

6. The new skyscraper …
   a) ☐ was planned in 2006.
   b) ☐ got another name in 2009.
   c) ☐ is called *Freedom Tower*.

7. The new building will be …
   a) ☐ 1 776 feet high.
   b) ☐ 1 676 feet high.
   c) ☐ 1 767 feet high.

8. Every year the moment of silence takes place at _____.

9. The terrorist attacks have not only influenced the _____ of
   the city but also the people's lives.

2 Hörverstehen Teil 2:
Queen Elizabeth II: Things You May Not Know 💿

*On April 21st, 1926, Queen Elizabeth II was born. In her more than 60 years on
the throne many generations in the United Kingdom grew up with her as their
monarch. But there are still some facts about her that are unknown to most people, which are presented in the following school podcast.*

> - *First read the tasks (1–9).*
> - *Then listen to the podcast about the Queen.*
> - *Tick the correct box or complete the sentences while you are listening.*
> - *Tick only **one** box.*
> - *At the end you will hear the podcast again.*
> - *Now read the tasks (1–9). You have 90 seconds to do this.*

1. When Elizabeth was born …
   a) ☐ her father wanted her to become Queen.
   b) ☐ nobody thought she would be Queen.
   c) ☐ her uncle got divorced.

2. All her family call her …
   a) ☐ Sausage.
   b) ☐ Queenie.
   c) ☐ Lilibet.

3. Elizabeth and Philip …
   a) ☐ wrote each other letters before their first meeting.
   b) ☐ got to know each other 60 years ago.
   c) ☐ met at a lunch for the first time.

4. Elizabeth did a job training as a _____.

5. The Queen …
   a) ☐ told Mrs Bush not to use her lipstick in public.
   b) ☐ always carries her lipstick with her.
   c) ☐ never uses lipstick in public.

6. A _____ broke into her house in 2003.

7. The Queen uses a mobile phone to write …
   a) ☐ facebook messages.
   b) ☐ twitter messages.
   c) ☐ text messages.

8. Queen Elizabeth was the first Royal who got a gold _____.

9. During a concert in 2012 the Queen had to protect her _____.

3 Leseverstehen

Charles Dickens: Voice of the poor

1 Britain is a nation of brilliant writers, but one of the most popular English novel-
ists in history is called Charles Dickens (1812–1870).
   At a time when Britain was the major economic and political power in the
world, Charles Dickens was the voice of the poor. He wrote classics like *Oliver*
5 *Twist* or *David Copperfield,* which describe the sad lives of poor working class
people in Britain's early Industrial Age. Dickens didn't invent his descriptions of
the dirt, poverty and child labour. He saw it all as he was growing up and it made
him want to fight against social injustice[1] and for social reforms.
   Dickens was born near Portsmouth on 7th February 1812, as the second of eight
10 children. His father was an office clerk who was paid quite well but always spent
more than he earned.
   Charles, a small sickly child, started school at the age of nine and soon discovered his love of reading. But then, at the age of eleven, this happy period in his
life came to a sudden end because his family was no longer able to pay for his
15 school education. But things got even worse: a few months later, his father was
locked up in *Marshalsea* prison in London with most of the family because he
couldn't pay his debts[2].
   To support his family, Charles was sent to work in Warren's Blacking Factory, a dirty, rat-infested[3] shoe polish factory in London, where he had to stick la-
20 bels on bottles six days a week from 8 a.m. to 8 p.m. for only one shilling[4] a day.
Each evening, Charles returned alone to his cheap rented room in Camden Town,
a three-mile walk from the factory. Sunday was the only day he could visit his
family at *Marshalsea* prison. A great deal of this extremely unhappy time of

Dickens' life is retold in his later writing, for example in *David Copperfield,* his
25 most autobiographical novel.

Luckily, after about a year, his father received an unexpected sum of money
and Charles could go back to school where he threw himself into the study of literature. He also wrote for the school newspaper and for a local newspaper. This
experience convinced him that he could earn his daily bread with his talent and
30 could guarantee a regular income which he could live on. At 15 he left school and
got a job as an office boy. But the work bored him. So he gave it up a few months
later and went into journalism, where he was soon a very successful reporter.

At the age of 24 Dickens started publishing his first novel, a satirical serial
called *The Pickwick Papers,* which was published in monthly parts for nearly two
35 years and became an immediate success. Thanks to this triumph, Dickens finally
became a full-time novelist giving the world around 20 wonderful novels, all of
them bestsellers.

Today, Dickens' novels are taught in schools around the world as examples of
brilliant writing. On 7th February 2012, Dickens' 200th birthday was remembered
40 throughout Britain. One of the main aims of the celebration was to encourage young
people to read. With their child protagonists such as *Oliver Twist* or *David Copperfield,* Dickens' works are just right for young readers.

Although living at a different time, far away from the problems Dickens' characters have to face, young readers meet characters who – despite their difference –
45 they can look up to for what they do. Through sharing the stories of Dickens' characters, their thoughts and experiences, young readers are made aware of social injustice and discover the similarities between today's world and Dickens' time.

1 injustice – unfairness
2 debts – money you have to pay back to s.o.
3 rat-infested – full of rats
4 one shilling – worth about € 4 today (At the time you could buy about 3 kilos of bread for one
   shilling.)

- *First read the text.*
- *Then do the tasks 1–9.*
- *For tasks 1, 3, 6 and 8 decide if the statements are true or false and tick the
  correct box. Then finish these sentences. You can quote from the text.*
- *For tasks 2, 4, 5 and 7 tick the correct box. Tick only* **one** *box for each task.*
- *For task 9 fill in the information.*

1. At the time of Dickens, Britain was an important country.
   This statement is
   a) ☒ true   b) ☐ false
   because the text says
   ll 3-4   At a time ... of the poor

2. Dickens wrote stories …
   a) ☒ about social reforms in Britain.
   b) ☐ that were a mirror of the unfairness of his time.
   c) ☐ he made up entirely himself.

3. Charles' father was good at managing his money.
   This statement is
   a) ☐ true   b) ☒ false
   because the text says
   ll. 8-11 for social reforms ... than he earned

4. When Charles Dickens was 11 years old he …
   a) ☐ developed a great interest in stories and books.
   b) ☐ spent his most wonderful time in London.
   c) ☒ had to interrupt his school education.

5. Charles Dickens' hard work as a factory boy …
   a) ☐ ended with visiting his parents every evening.
   b) ☐ is described in one of his later books.
   c) ☒ meant producing bottles the whole week.

6. When he was still very young, Dickens realized that he could earn his money
   through writing.
   This statement is
   a) ☒ true   b) ☐ false
   because the text says

   _____

7. Dickens' *Pickwick Papers* were …
   a) ☒ the young author's first success as a full-time writer.
   b) ☐ soon followed by other very successful novels.
   c) ☐ bestsellers after only two years.

8. On his 200th birthday, a celebration was organized to improve pupils' interest in books.
   This statement is
   a) ☒ true   b) ☐ false
   because the text says

   _____

9. Charles Dickens' stories are still relevant for young people today. Give two reasons:
   a) _____
   b) _____

Zweiter Prüfungsteil: Wortschatz – Schreiben

Punk for a month

4 Wortschatz: *Teenage years*

The following text (sentences 1–13) is about young people.

> - *Sentences 1, 2, 4, 5, 8, 10, 11: fill in suitable words.*
> - *Sentences 3, 6, 7, 9, 12, 13: tick the correct box (there is only **one** correct answer).*

1. Young people ___between___ 12 and 18 are usually called teenagers.

2. Teenagers are not children anymore, but they are not yet ___adult___ either.

3. In a new …
   a) ☐ election   b) ☐ opinion
   c) ☒ survey   d) ☐ roundabout
   young people say that the people they talk to first when they have a problem are their friends.

4. It is usually most important to young people to be ___they supported___ by peers, that means by other young people of their age.

5. That's why many people ___are part of___ a clique of friends.

6. Young people often think that acting cool makes them popular …
   a) ☐ by   b) ☒ for
   c) ☐ with   d) ☐ to
   their peers.

7. Quite a number of young people copy their friends' hairstyles or the …
   a) ☐ art   b) ☒ way
   c) ☐ kind   d) ☐ type
   they dress even if secretly they have a different taste.

8. These young people just do not have enough ___*money*___
   to follow their individual style.

9. It is typical of many young people to wear the …
   a) ☒ latest   b) ☐ final
   c) ☐ freshest   d) ☐ youngest
   fashion.

10. So they ___*spend*___ a lot of time shopping for clothes.

11. Wearing the "right" things is important. Some young people even _*bully*_
    others if they don't.

12. In other words, young people often judge others by their …
    a) ☐ outlook.   b) ☐ lookout.
    c) ☐ views.   d) ☒ looks.

13. As a result, teenagers sometimes even …
    a) ☐ put up   b) ☒ break up
    c) ☐ run off   d) ☐ get on
    with friends because of their outer appearance.

5 Schreiben

Punk for a month

1 … "Here I am," I thought, "Julie Hamilton, straight[1] American grade 11 student. Looks – plain[2]. Parties, going out – forget about it! Boyfriend – only in my fantasies. My life is dead boring … I need a change!" …

Robbie and Tanya, two girls from my gym class, came in. They were very
5 punk, but somehow they had always fascinated me. … PUNK! … I would become a punk! … I was going to surprise everyone.

The next day I called my best friend Anne, who went to another school. "What?" she asked amazed. "You heard me. By tomorrow I'll be a punk. I'm sick of being called a goody-goody!" "Okay," she said, "if that's your decision. But I
10 think you are making a great mistake." She made me promise that I'd only be a punk for one month – only until my hair grew out. I agreed. After a month I would stop.

I thought Mom would kill me, but she must have been too tired to argue with me. She just said: "It's your life. If you think it's important, go right ahead. But
15 if it gets you into trouble, don't come crying to me."

I went to the hairstylist straight away and got a punk haircut. Then I dyed my hair green in front. And I went to a second-hand shop where I spent nearly all my savings on a punk-style outfit.

The next morning I was nervous and a little scared. I had put on punk-style
20 make-up and I wore a purple mini, a black and purple striped shirt, a black leather jacket, high-heeled shoes and large black earrings.

I took a deep breath when I stepped into the school building. "It's silly to worry," I told myself. "Nothing has changed, except your appearance." Robbie told me I looked terrific. I got a few other compliments, too, but most people were star-
25 ing at me.

My first chance to talk to my clique came during lunch period. Patty, Ellen, Kelly, Stacy and Cathy were already sitting at the table we shared every day. No one said a word as I approached. I sat down and looked at them. For five minutes nothing happened. Finally I said: "What's the matter?" Cathy spoke first. "Are
30 you going to look like that for a long time?" "I like it," I said ... "It's not really you, Julie," Ellen said. No one replied. No one looked my way.

"Fine," I said angrily. "I'm not going to bother you any more. I'll just sit with Robbie and Tanya. What a fool I was to think you were really friends!" I stomped off.

35 Robbie and Tanya were glad to see me. I held back my tears and tried to enjoy myself.

The next few days were the best days of my life. People I didn't know stopped me in the streets, to talk to me or compliment me – Robbie's and Tanya's friends of course. But it wasn't only punks. And I got a few friendly looks from boys
40 who had never given me a second look before.

Soon nobody was staring at me anymore. Teachers and students had got used to me. My ex-friends, however, seemed to take every opportunity to try to hurt me. One day, they were all standing by their lockers. When I arrived, Kelly suddenly said to them rather loudly: "Hey, guys, I'm having a party this Saturday. Can you
45 all come?" "Terrific! Who are you inviting?" Cathy asked seemingly innocent[3]. "Oh, everyone *normal,*" Kelly informed her as loudly as before. That did it.

Anne came over the next afternoon and reminded me of my promise to stop after one month. "I'm no longer sure if I want to", I said.

adapted from: Lynn Steiner: Punk for a month. In: Merlyn's Pen I, Issue 3

Annotations
1 straight – normal, conventional
2 plain – ordinary, not very beautiful or attractive
3 seemingly innocent – doing as if she didn't mean to hurt her

1. **Describe** how Julie changes her outer appearance and how her friend, Anne, and her mother react to her decision to turn punk.

2. **Explain** why Julie decides to turn punk and why she is unsure about going back to "normal" in the end.

3. You have a choice here. Choose **one** of the following tasks:

   a) PUNK is an unusual lifestyle.
   What **risks** and what **chances** are there for young people who are not like everybody else? Give reasons and examples.

   or

   b) After a month, Anne writes to Julie and tries to convince her to change back to "normal".
   Write Anne's **email** using the following ideas:
   – Anne's observations of things that have changed,
   – Anne's feelings about Julie's new look,
   – possible consequences Julie's new style can have on her life.

Lösungsvorschläge

Erster Prüfungsteil: Hörverstehen – Leseverstehen

Mittlerer Schulabschluss – Haupttermin

Wichtige Hinweise: Alle Texte, die im Folgenden zu hören sind, werden zweimal vorgespielt. Vor dem ersten Hören hast du Zeit, dich mit den Aufgaben vertraut zu machen. Der Hörverstehenstest besteht aus zwei Teilen.

---

1 Hörverstehen Teil 1: *Memories of 9/11*

---

*On September 11th, 2001, terrorists directed two planes into the World Trade Center in New York. Lots of people died and the Twin Towers were completely destroyed. Chloe Morton from USspotRadio is reporting live from the 9/11 Tribute Center. First read the tasks (1–9). Then listen to the report. Tick the correct box or complete the sentences while you are listening. Tick only **one** box. At the end you will hear the report again. Now read the tasks (1–9). You have 90 seconds to do this.*
Now listen to the report and do the tasks.

---

1 CHLOE: This is *USspotRadio* and I'm Chloe Morton live from New York. September 11 is a special day for us New Yorkers, even eleven years after the terrorist attacks. Volunteer tour guides who have been directly affected by the events of September 11 because they are survivors, have lost loved ones or were res-

5   cue workers at the time, share their stories and personal experiences.
I'm here, right in front of the National September 11 Memorial which was built so that we always remember the nearly 3 000 people killed in the terror attacks.
Set in the footprints of where the Twin Towers once stood, there are two enor-

10 mous pools now with the highest waterfalls made by man. The names of the nearly 3 000 victims have been written in a wall along the pools.
WITNESS: I think the plan to arrange the names that way, based on the idea where the victims were and who they were with, or next to colleagues they worked with, instead of placing them alphabetically or chronologically is a very mean-

15 ingful solution.
CHLOE: It's not only lots of New Yorkers but also tourists from all over the world who come here to remember the dead.
WITNESS: I grew up in New York ... and I don't live here anymore. For me the skyline still looks ... kind of strange, I still miss those great towers ...

₂₀ CHLOE: In fact the city has changed and a lot of reconstruction work has taken place. A new skyscraper, called *One World Trade Center,* has replaced the former Twin Towers. Its role will be similar. Soon there will be huge office areas but also a lot of shops and restaurants. There will be an observation deck again with a fantastic view over New York.

₂₅ When construction work started in 2006, that new building was called *Freedom Tower.* In March 2009, however, the name was changed to *One World Trade Center* for easier identification. Of course it's a symbol of our nation's strength and triumph over terrorism. With its 1 776 feet, it is again the tallest building here in New York and the highest in the US.

₃₀ As incredible as it sounds, this sad event brings lots of people together. Every year hundreds of people come together in Times Square, carrying US flags. There is a moment of silence at 08:46 am, the exact time when the first airplane hit the tower.

WITNESS: The events of 9/11 did not only change the face of our city, they also af-₃₅ fected our lives.

CHLOE: The attacks have left a serious impression on young people and many of them are now trying to make the world a better place.

Chloe Morton for *USspotRadio,* New York.

Now listen to the report again and check your answers.

---

1. … (personal) experiences.
   ✔ *Hinweis:* "… *they are survivors, have lost loved ones or were rescue workers at the time, share their stories and personal experiences." (Z. 4/5)*

2. … (enormous) pools.
   ✔ *Hinweis:* "*Set in the footprints of where the Twin Towers once stood, there are two enormous pools now …" (Z. 9/10)*

3. c) … next to their colleagues' names.
   ✔ *Hinweis:* "… *arrange the names that way, based on the idea where the victims were and who they were with, or next to colleagues they worked with …"* *(Z. 12–14)*

4. c) … remembers the Twin Towers with sadness.
   ✔ *Hinweis:* "*For me the skyline still looks … kind of strange, I still miss those great towers …" (Z. 18/19)*

5. … shops …
   ✔ *Hinweis:* "*Soon there will be huge office areas but also a lot of shops and restaurants." (Z. 22/23)*

6. b) … got another name in 2009.
   Hinweis: "*In March 2009, however, the name was changed to* One World Trade Center *for easier identification.*" (Z. 26/27)

7. a) … 1 776 feet high.
   Hinweis: "*With its 1 776 feet, it is again the tallest building here in New York …*" (Z. 28/29)

8. … 8:46 am/Times Square.
   Hinweis: "*Every year hundreds of people come together in Times Square, carrying US flags. There is a moment of silence at 08:46 am …*" (Z. 30–32)

9. … face …
   Hinweis: "*The events of 9/11 did not only change the face of our city, they also affected our lives.*" (Z. 34/35)

2   Hörverstehen Teil 2: *Queen Elizabeth II: Things You May Not Know*

> *On April 21st, 1926, Queen Elizabeth II was born. In her more than 60 years on the throne many generations in the United Kingdom grew up with her as their monarch. But there are still some facts about her that are unknown to most people, which are presented in the following school podcast. First read the tasks (1–9). Then listen to the podcast about the Queen. Tick the correct box or complete the sentences while you are listening. Tick only* **one** *box. At the end you will hear the podcast again. Now read the tasks (1–9). You have 90 seconds to do this. Now listen to the podcast and do the tasks.*

1 Hello everybody and welcome to *classpod,* your weekly school podcast. We recently celebrated Queen Elizabeth's Diamond Jubilee and therefore our topic today will be the Queen and her life. Everybody thinks they know a lot about the Queen, but is this really the case? Listen to what we found out!

5   When Elizabeth Alexandra Mary Windsor was born, nobody expected she would one day be queen. She was only third in line for the throne. When her uncle, Edward, wanted to marry a divorced woman, he gave the crown to Elizabeth's father, who died in 1952.

These're still mostly well known facts, but let's now turn to something you may
10 not know …

Did you know that she's got a nickname? Guess what it is. – Lizzy? Elli? Or maybe even Queenie? Wrong! She's called "Lilibet" by family members. But her husband has another pet name for her: SAUSAGE! *Err …,* we wouldn't advise you to address Her Majesty that way if you ever met her!

¹⁵ This leads us to the interesting story about Elizabeth and her husband, Prince Philip. Elizabeth was only 13 when she met him for the first time. Philip was invited for lunch and she immediately fell in love with him. The two teenagers quickly began exchanging letters. Elizabeth never wanted any other man but Philip, and in 2007 they celebrated their 60 years' wedding anniversary.

²⁰ Now to business: You might think a queen doesn't have experience of a proper job, but that's not true! During World War II she got her hands dirty joining the Military Service in 1945. There she trained as a mechanic and worked as a driver although she hasn't even got a driving license.

What about her job in public? You might know that the Queen goes nowhere ²⁵ without her handbag. Inside she keeps her trusty lipstick, which she's not afraid to use in public. Former First Lady of the United States Laura Bush once did the same and said: "The Queen told me it was all right to do it."

We all know that Queen Elizabeth always behaves like a lady, but she's brave as well! In 1982, when a stalker entered her bedroom, she remained calm, having ³⁰ a conversation with the man until the police arrived. Again, in 2003, someone managed to enter Buckingham Palace without permission. He was a journalist who later reported that the Queen used Tupperware boxes for her cornflakes.

Did you know that the Queen's a very modern monarch? According to an insider, she started using a cell phone to text messages to her grandchildren. And with ³⁵ her own YouTube channel, Facebook page, and Twitter handle she's arrived in the digital age.

You surely know that the Queen is very famous, but did you know that she got a music award? In 2002 she celebrated her Golden Jubilee with a pop concert. Many people bought a CD of this concert, and thus Queen Elizabeth became the first ⁴⁰ member of the Royal Family to receive a gold disc. Another concert was arranged on her Diamond Jubilee in 2012. But this time close observers noticed that the Queen protected her ears with earplugs! Maybe Robbie Williams was a bit too loud for Her Majesty …

Now listen to the podcast again and check your answers.

Ende des Hörverstehenstests.

---

1. b) … nobody thought she would be Queen.
   Hinweis: "*When Elizabeth Alexandra Mary Windsor was born, nobody expected she would one day be queen.*" *(Z. 5/6)*

2. c) … Lilibet.
   Hinweis: "*She's called 'Lilibet' by family members.*" *(Z. 12)*

3. c) ... met at a lunch for the first time.
   Hinweis: "*Elizabeth was only 13 when she met him for the first time. Philip was invited for lunch ...*" (Z. 16/17)

4. ... mechanic.
   Hinweis: "*There she trained as a mechanic ...*" (Z. 22)

5. b) ... always carries her lipstick with her.
   Hinweis: "*... the Queen goes nowhere without her handbag. Inside she keeps her trusty lipstick ...*" (Z. 24/25)

6. ... journalist ...
   Hinweis: "*Again, in 2003, someone managed to enter Buckingham Palace without permission. He was a journalist ...*" (Z. 30/31)

7. c) ... text messages.
   Hinweis: "*According to an insider, she started using a cell phone to text messages to her grandchildren.*" (Z. 33/34)

8. ... disc.
   Hinweis: "*... and thus Queen Elizabeth became the first member of the Royal Family to receive a gold disc.*" (Z. 39/40)

9. ... ears.
   Hinweis: "*Another concert was arranged on her Diamond Jubilee in 2012. But this time close observers noticed that the Queen protected her ears with earplugs!*" (Z. 40–42)

3 Leseverstehen

1. a) true
   "... Britain was the major economic and political power in the world ..."
   Hinweis: Z. 3/4

2. b) ... that were a mirror of the unfairness of his time.
   Hinweis: "*He wrote classics like* Oliver Twist *or* David Copperfield, *which describe the sad lives of poor working class people in Britain's early Industrial Age.*" (Z. 4–6)

3. b) false
   "... [he] spent more than he earned."
   Hinweis: Z. 10/11

4. c) ... had to interrupt his school education.
    Hinweis: "But then, at the age of eleven, this happy period in his life came to a sudden end because his family was no longer able to pay for his school education." (Z. 13–15)

5. b) ... is described in one of his later books.
    Hinweis: "A great deal of this extremely unhappy time of Dickens' life is retold in his later writing ..." (Z. 23/24)

6. a) true
    "This experience convinced him that he could earn his daily bread with his talent ..."
    Hinweis: Z. 28/29

7. b) ... soon followed by other very successful novels.
    Hinweis: "Thanks to this triumph, Dickens finally became a full-time novelist giving the world around 20 wonderful novels ..." (Z. 35/36)

8. a) true
    "... encourage young people to read."
    Hinweis: Z. 40/41

9. a) They can look up to the characters.
    Hinweis: "... young readers meet characters who ... they can look up to for what they do." (Z. 44/45)

    b) They are made aware of injustice. / They discover the similarities between today's world and Dickens' time.
    Hinweis: "... young readers are made aware of social injustice and discover the similarities between today's world and Dickens' time." (Z. 46/47)

Punk for a month

4. Wortschatz: *Teenage years*

1. between

2. adult(s) / grown-up(s) / of age / ...

3. c) survey

4. accepted / respected / supported / liked / ...

5. belong to / are a member of / are part of / join ...

6. c) with

7. b) way

8. courage / self-confidence / (inner) strength / strength of character / ...

9. a) latest

10. spend

11. discriminate against / pick on / bully / make fun of / laugh at / ...

12. d) looks

13. b) break up

5   Schreiben

*⊘ **Hinweis:** Bei den Schreibaufgaben ist nicht vorgegeben, wie lang deine Texte genau sein sollen. Du solltest aber bei den Aufgaben 5.1 und 5.2 nicht weniger als 80 Wörter und bei 5.3 und 5.4 nicht weniger als 120 Wörter schreiben. Wenn du weniger schreibst, besteht die Gefahr, dass du nicht alle Aspekte der Aufgabenstellung berücksichtigt hast. Lies dir am Ende auf jeden Fall alles noch einmal aufmerksam durch und verbessere Fehler.*
Die Aufgaben 1 und 2 beziehen sich direkt auf den Lesetext. Um zu wissen, nach welchen Informationen du im Text suchen musst, ist es wichtig, dass du dir die Aufgabenstellungen genau durchliest. Danach gehst du den Text noch einmal aufmerksam durch und markierst die relevanten Textstellen farbig. So übersiehst du keine wichtigen Details.

1. *Hinweis: Du kannst hier Formulierungen aus dem Lesetext übernehmen. Achte aber darauf, nicht einfach nur Sätze aus dem Text aneinanderzureihen. Es ist wichtig, dass dein Text insgesamt eine Einheit bildet. Verbinde die Sätze also sinnvoll miteinander und verwende möglichst eigenständige Formulierungen.*

Julie goes to a hairdresser and gets a punk haircut. Afterwards she dyes her hair green at the front. Next she goes to a second-hand shop and buys a punk-style outfit. The day after, she puts on punk-style make-up and a purple mini, a black and purple striped shirt, a black leather jacket, high-heeled shoes, and large black earrings.

Anne is worried about Julie's decision. She thinks that her friend is making a big mistake and persuades her to stop after a month. Surprisingly, Julie's mother is more relaxed about it. She accepts her daughter's decision and tells her to carry on if she thinks it is important. But she also tells her not to complain if she gets into trouble because of her new look.　　*124 words*

2. Julie thinks that she is not attractive. She doesn't have a boyfriend and she believes that her life is boring and conventional. She therefore decides that she wants to make a change in her life. She is sick of being a good little girl.

In the end Julie is not sure about keeping the promise she made to her friend Anne and going back to "normal". The punk days have been the best days of her life. People stop her in the street to talk to her or compliment her on the way she looks. What's more, boys actually pay attention to her, something that has never happened before. Another reason is that her former friends are still rude to her because of her changed appearance. Julie doesn't want to accept that. Turning back into a "normal" girl would mean giving in.

142 words

3. a) *Hinweis: Bei dieser Aufgabe musst du sowohl über positive als auch über negative Seiten eines Lebens als Punk schreiben. Dabei darfst du aus deiner Perspektive argumentieren und kannst dir aussuchen, welcher Seite du zustimmst. Achte darauf, deine Argumente durch konkrete Beispiele zu untermauern.*

Punk is a very exceptional lifestyle. People who only judge you by your looks will probably not understand you. This can cause a lot of problems, especially when you apply for a job. Employers usually have strict ideas about dress codes. As a punk, you could never work as a receptionist in a hotel or in a bank, for example.

In addition, you might fall in with the wrong sort of people, the kind who would lead you onto the wrong track. In big cities, you can see punks sitting in the streets, many of them drinking alcohol, taking drugs, asking for money, and sleeping under bridges away from their families. This way of life is often a road of no return.

On the other hand, becoming a punk can also turn you into a confident person. With their unusual outfits, punks demonstrate their dislike of conformity. They are individualists and rebels. Our society needs rebels who criticize when something is wrong. Like Julie, you will get a lot of attention from people. You are someone special because you have a message.

182 words

b) *Hinweis: Hier musst du eine E-Mail schreiben. Vergiss also die Anrede und die Verabschiedung nicht. Gehe auf alle Punkte in der Aufgabe ein.*

Dear Julie,

I've waited a really long time before writing this email. Four weeks have passed, and I get the feeling that you aren't going to keep your promise and stop being a punk.

I'm worried because so many things have changed now. A lot of your former friends avoid hanging out with you. I was sad when Kelly didn't invite you to her party. It was fun, and I missed having you there. And, worst of all, Kelly hurt you by making sure everyone heard that she'd only invite "normal" people. It makes me sad and angry when other people hurt you. You are my best friend, and I miss the days we used to spend together having fun.

If you carry on like this, you'll lose even more of your friends. You'll end up in isolation. But I'll always be your friend and stand by you.

Both of us will have to find a job in the near future, and it would be great if we could support each other in that. But if you keep on being a punk, you'll definitely have a lot of problems finding a job you like.

Julie, please think of your future and your best friend.

Please write soon.

Anne

207 words

Erster Prüfungsteil: Hörverstehen – Leseverstehen

1 Hörverstehen Teil 1: *J. K. Rowling – a success story*

She is an international star and has fascinated young and old readers with her fantasy world of magic: J. K. Rowling and her Harry Potter series. In a radio interview, Naomi finds out more about the British writer's success story with the help of her guest, Jeff.

- *First read the tasks (1–9).*
- *Then listen to the interview.*
- *Tick the correct box or complete the sentences while you are listening.*
- *Tick only **one** box.*
- *At the end you will hear the interview again.*
- *Now read the tasks (1–9). You have 90 seconds to do this.*
- *Now listen to the interview and do the tasks.*

1. Rowling's books …
   a) ☐ are published in 400 languages.
   b) ☐ were sold more than 200,000 times.
   c) ☐ have been translated into 60 languages.

2. Becoming a writer was …
   a) ☐ Rowling's childhood dream.
   b) ☐ the plan of Rowling's parents.
   c) ☐ just a job after her apprenticeship.

3. Rowling invented the story for Harry Potter on a _____.

4. Rowling got the idea for her main character's name, Potter, from a
   _____.

5. Using the initials J. K. for her books is …
   a) ☐ a strategy to get more readers.
   b) ☐ a personal choice to keep some privacy.
   c) ☐ a reference to Rowling's grandmother's last name.

6. Before her career started, Rowling ...
   a) ☐ was jobless in Portugal.
   b) ☐ suffered a family loss.
   c) ☐ had little time to write her book.

7. Writing in a café ...
   a) ☐ gave her the idea for Hogwarts.
   b) ☐ became quite expensive after a while.
   c) ☐ helped her to invent interesting characters.

8. It is hard to believe that _____ did not show any interest in her first book at first.

9. Jeff thinks Rowling is a bestselling author because of her various
   _____.

2 Hörverstehen Teil 2: *English – a changing language* 💿

Jared Warren and Kim Dakuma, two senior students at Woodpeck High, are doing a presentation on "English – a changing language" in class.

- *First read the tasks of the quiz (1–9).*
- *Then listen to the presentation.*
- *Tick the correct box or complete the sentences while you are listening.*
- *Tick only **one** box.*
- *At the end you will hear the presentation again.*
- *Now read the tasks (1–9). You have 90 seconds to do this.*
- *Now listen to the presentation and do the tasks of the quiz.*

1. English people will never _____ of words because the language changes constantly.

2. Early modern English ...
   a) ☐ is quite similar to German.
   b) ☐ dates back to a thousand years ago.
   c) ☐ was influenced by W. Shakespeare.

3. When _____ was introduced, the English language started to standardize.

4. English is spoken …
   a) ☐ in 45 different countries.
   b) ☐ by 340 million native speakers.
   c) ☐ by 1.5 billion people worldwide.

5. English goes global in _____, science and research.

6. English is used in …
   a) ☐ some scientific documents.
   b) ☐ 3/4 of postal communication.
   c) ☐ 25 different varieties worldwide.

7. In English vocabulary you have …
   a) ☐ 340,000 officially accepted words.
   b) ☐ 2,000 words for everyday communication.
   c) ☐ 8,000 words after 4 years of learning English.

8. The English language changes daily because people _____
   words for example in text messages.

9. Few people know that …
   a) ☐ "stewardess" is typed with only the right hand.
   b) ☐ there is only one rhyme with "month" or "angel".
   c) ☐ "goodbye" comes from the greeting "God be with you".

3   Leseverstehen

One world – different cultures? Festivals spreading around the world!

1 **A** When Irish and Scots emigrated to America in the 19th century no one
would have expected that their Halloween celebration would one day become
one of the probably most well-known immigrant traditions. Across the globe
millions of people dress up in fancy costumes to celebrate "All Hallow-Eves"!
5 Unfortunately, only few know the idea and tradition behind it. Nowadays people only like to buy funny decorations, crazy costumes and lots of sweets. Halloween parties are offered to the public in every town and village.

B As the English-speaking world becomes increasingly colourful and diverse,
Halloween is not the only popular festival in the world anymore. More and
10 more British and American people join in festivals of immigrant culture that
are not originally theirs.

C One of these is *Diwali*, which was brought to the English world by Indian
immigrants. *Diwali* means "a row of lamps", which are lit to suggest the victory of good over evil, light over darkness and knowledge over ignorance. The

15 festival also marks a new beginning of family values, and it represents values of love, reflection, forgiveness and knowledge. In India lots of small lamps and candles are lit and fireworks are let off everywhere. People clean and decorate their houses and give each other presents.

D The popularity of this event in England's capital, with the support of the
20 office of the Mayor of London, has increased enormously. Since 2002 mass celebrations in Trafalgar Square have been held every year with English people coming from different cultural backgrounds. They meet and celebrate *Diwali* together with a colourful mix of music, dance, live performances, displays and food stalls. And what is important, too, the celebrations in Trafalgar Square
25 are free and open to all. The idea for "*Diwali* in Trafalgar Square" was born when three friends had a "collective dream": a vision of a harmonious and grand mass celebration by London's multi-cultural community. They wanted to reach as many Londoners as possible, while still keeping the true spirit of *Diwali* alive.

30 **E** In the United States, too, with an increasing Indian population, *Diwali* is becoming more important year after year. *Diwali* was first celebrated in the White House in 2003. Later, in 2007, the former president George W. Bush and the Congress of the United States officially recognized the religious and historical importance of *Diwali*. In 2009, one day before his first visit to India
35 as the President of the United States, Barack Obama made an official statement sharing best wishes with "those celebrating *Diwali*". People from the Asian continent living in the US celebrate *Diwali* in different parts of the US, just as in India.

F Traces of immigrant culture can also be found in important sporting events
40 or pop culture. For example the Color Run™[1], a unique paint race, has become the single largest 5K event series (five kilometre races) in the US. It combines the Hindu spring festival of colours *Holi* which celebrates the beginning of the new season after winter with a celebration of health, happiness, and individuality, bringing people from all races and ages together to create a five kilometre
45 painting of colourful fun. Just like in the *Holi* celebration the athletes are powdered in bright colours every few kilometres by spectators on the road. The paint race also focuses on giving things back to people who are having a difficult time: the organisation chooses a local charity in each city it visited, and has raised donations[2] for over 60 local and national social projects in 2012.
50 The Color Run™ has also reached Germany. The organizers call „Lauf dich bunt!" the craziest 5K run in Germany.

What a colourful world we live in!

1 TM – trademark
2 to raise donations – to collect money for a charity project

- *First read the text.*
- *Then do the tasks 1–10.*
- *For tasks 1, 2, 5, 6, 7 and 9 tick the correct box. Tick only **one** box for each task.*
- *For tasks 3, 4, and 8 fill in the information.*
- *For task 10 match the headlines (1–6) to the paragraphs A–F.*

1. Today's fans of Halloween have …
    a) ☐ discovered the origin of Halloween again.
    b) ☐ turned Halloween into a commercial party.
    c) ☐ made Halloween the most famous foreign tradition worldwide.

2. Foreign traditions and festivals …
    a) ☐ are overtaking Halloween's popularity.
    b) ☐ become different in the immigrant country.
    c) ☐ change cultural practices of the English-speaking world.

3. What does Diwali stand for? Give two examples from the text:
    a) _____
    b) _____

4. Diwali celebrations in London connect people. Prove from the text and give two examples:
    a) _____
    b) _____

5. In bringing Diwali to London, a group of friends wanted to …
    a) ☐ organize a spiritual mass celebration.
    b) ☐ celebrate a huge and peaceful festival.
    c) ☐ bring a great number of religions together.

6. Diwali …
    a) ☐ was given official status in 2007.
    b) ☐ has been celebrated throughout America since 2003.
    c) ☐ was honoured by Barack Obama on his trip to the Asian continent in 2009.

7. The Color Run^{TM} …
    a) ☐ is a popular and crazy social event.
    b) ☐ is part of a Hindu winter festival.
    c) ☐ is a unique American sports competition.

8. During the Color Run™ people can do different things. Give two examples from the text:

a) _____

b) _____

9. By summing up *What a colourful world we live in!* (l. 52) the author wants to express that …

a) ☐ the world is constantly changing.

b) ☐ people have great and crazy ideas.

c) ☐ he welcomes the influence of different cultures.

10. Match the headlines 1–6 to the paragraphs A–F.

	Headlines	Paragraphs
1	Having a good time together	
2	A colourful and charitable competition	
3	New reasons to celebrate	
4	Prominent support	
5	Famous tradition	
6	Celebrating what is important in life	

Zweiter Prüfungsteil: Wortschatz – Schreiben

Miss Liberty

4   Wortschatz: *Teen advice*

In Teen Magazine young people can ask for advice. The following text is a piece of advice given to a teenage reader.

- *Sentences 1, 4, 5, 8, 9 and 10: fill in suitable words.*
- *Sentences 2, 3, and 7: tick the correct box (there is only **one** correct answer)*
- *Sentence 6: tick the correct box (there is only **one** correct answer) and complete the sentence.*

1. Don't panic! It's normal to feel confused from time to time. Growing up is a period of _____ feelings!

2. A lot of young people are …
   a) ☐ worried　　　　b) ☐ afraid
   c) ☐ panicked　　　 d) ☐ frightened
   about what other people think about them.

3. Teenage years are a time of great …
   a) ☐ action　　　　 b) ☐ conflict
   c) ☐ animation　　　d) ☐ liveliness
   between adults and growing-ups.

4. Just to be accepted by peers you shouldn't _____ against everything your parents want you to do.

5. It's important for you to find out what your real _____ is.

6. You shouldn't just …
   a) ☐ copy　　　　　 b) ☐ look like
   c) ☐ resemble　　　 d) ☐ reproduce
   your friends' _____ and outfit especially when you don't like them!

7. What you should always keep in mind is that …
   a) ☐ destroying　　　b) ☐ undoing
   c) ☐ answering　　　d) ☐ solving
   a conflict is difficult both for adults and for you.

8. This is why you should remind adults from time to time that it's important for you to make your own _____ and accept the
   _____.

9. Provoking people who are _____ for your safety and happiness only makes things more complicated for you.

10. Remember, the real world can be a cruel place sometimes, and one day you'll be happy to face it with the _____ of an adult.

5 Schreiben

Miss Liberty

1 It all started one night in 1975 when Mom – she's an artist plus she has a business degree – got her great idea about designing and selling little toy puppets[1] for the 200th birthday of the Statue of Liberty. Mom really made a lot of money from those puppets, and so she opened pretty big savings accounts[2] for all of us
5 and told us when we were sixteen we could do ANYTHING WE WANTED with our money, and when I said, "Like go to Paris for the summer and play my guitar on the Boulevard Saint Michel?" she said, "Sure, you bet[3]."
So that's the whole background, but it was this spring that the story really starts. Looking up from practicing *Hotel California* on my guitar I said, "So, Mom,
10 now that I'm sixteen, this summer I'm going to Paris." And Mom said, "So, Monica, now that you're sixteen, you must be out of your mind!"
So the argument was endless, and Nina and Toby and MiniMac actually climbed up a tree to watch us through the window screaming at each other about how "you said I could" and "I need you around this summer, Monica," and "This is
15 like having a third world dictatorship!" and then MiniMac actually fell out of the tree and the twins started screaming and Mom rushed outside yelling, "You see! You see why I need you?"
I took it up with Dad, and he just said, "Monica, if your mother says no, it's no."
Back in my room I screamed at the top of my lungs. I had a puppet of the Statue
20 of Liberty in my room and I reached for it and then I had this BRILLIANT idea which I put into action the next morning. When I went down to breakfast that morning, I was dressed in a gray sheet, with a tinfoil[4] Statue-of-Liberty-like crown, and I held a book and a torch (flashlight, that is). Toasts and coffee cups paused on their way to mouths as I nodded hello to my family at the breakfast
25 table, took a banana, and made my way out of the door.
Imitating the Statue of Liberty is easy. Really. You hold your book in one hand, raise your flashlight into the air in the other and stare straight ahead. I took my position on the walk that leads to our front door. After a while Dad opened the front door and strolled out, lighting a cigarette. He threw the match away and
30 looked at me for a moment.
"So, what's this all about?"
"Protest."
"Protest for what?"
"For going to Paris."
35 "Your mother says you aren't going."
"I say I am."
"Oh."

He chucked his cigarette away and went inside. – The door opened again and
Mom came out.

40 "This is foolish, Monica."

"I don't agree."

"It's a school day."

"So what?"

My flashlight arm was beginning to tire.

45 "How long are you planning to stand here?"

"Until you and Dad keep your promise."

The Brillsteins' door opened and Mr. Brillstein came out.

"Good morning! So, Halloween already?"

"Just a misunderstanding," Mom explained.

50 "It's a protest, Mr. Brillstein. I'm going to imitate the Statue of Liberty until I
gain[5] my own liberty".

"Political action – that's good in a young person," Mr. Brillstein said and got
into his car.

Mom went inside.

55 I stood there on the front walk for the rest of the morning. Mom brought me a
sandwich at noon, but didn't say anything.

Adapted from "The Statue of Liberty Factory" by Jennifer Armstrong. Published in STAY TRUE:
SHORT STORIES FOR STRONG GIRLS compiled by Marilyn Singer. Scholastic Inc./Scholastic
Press. Copyright © 1998 by Jennifer Armstrong. Reprinted by permission.

1 puppet – little doll
2 savings account – here: money that you save in a bank
3 You bet! – expression which is used to say that you are quite certain that sth. is true
4 tinfoil – metal made into very thin sheets that is used for wrapping food, etc.
5 to gain – here: to get

- *Read the tasks carefully.*
- *Write complete sentences.*
- *Make sure to write about **all** the aspects presented in each task.*

---

1. **Describe** Monica's problem and how she tries to solve it.

2. In the text it says: "So the argument was endless, … " (l. 12).
   Explain how Monica and her mother feel about the trip to Paris and why
   they feel the way they do.

3. You have a choice here. Choose **one** of the following tasks:

   a) "You should never break a promise."
      Comment on the statement from your point of view and include the fol-
      lowing aspects:

– Discuss the pros and cons of this statement.
– Give reasons and examples.

or

b) After a long night spent outside in the front garden dressed up as the *Statue of Liberty* Monica enters the kitchen the next morning. Only her mother is already awake waiting with a hot breakfast.
Write a suitable ending in the way the story is told and include the following aspects:
– their reactions to what happened,
– the reasons for their behavior,
– the deal they make about the trip to Paris.

Lösungsvorschläge

Erster Prüfungsteil: Hörverstehen – Leseverstehen

Mittlerer Schulabschluss – Haupttermin

Wichtige Hinweise: Alle Texte, die im Folgenden zu hören sind, werden zweimal vorgespielt. Vor dem ersten Hören wird Zeit gegeben, sich mit den Aufgaben vertraut zu machen. Der Hörverstehenstest besteht aus zwei Teilen.

1 Hörverstehen Teil 1: *J. K. Rowling – a success story*

*She is an international star and has fascinated young and old readers with her fantasy world of magic: J. K. Rowling and her Harry Potter series. In a radio interview, Naomi finds out more about the British writer's success story with the help of her guest, Jeff. First read the tasks (1–9). Then listen to the interview. Tick the correct box or complete the sentences while you are listening. Tick only **one** box. At the end you will hear the interview again. Now read the tasks (1–9). You have 90 seconds to do this.*
Now listen to the interview and do the tasks.

1 NAOMI: This is Naomi from Radio Escape with our popular show *Celebrity Talk!* With me in the studio is Jeff Brown. Hi Jeff.
JEFF: Hi there.
NAOMI: Jeff, today we're talking about one of the greatest children's fiction
5   writers ... J. K. Rowling.

JEFF: So true! What would our world be like without Mrs Rowling? Her books have been sold more than 400 million times in over 200 countries and 60 languages. Both adults and kids simply love her fantasy world.

NAOMI: Jeff, this is a real success story. Tell us, when did Mrs Rowling get the
10 idea to write?

JEFF: Actually, she'd been writing since she was six! Writing novels was Rowling's childhood dream. But, you know, her parents thought this would not lead to a proper job. They wanted her to start an apprenticeship. She, however, wanted to study English literature. And that's what she did secretly!

15 NAOMI: Really?! And how did she come up with the idea of *Harry Potter?*

JEFF: Well, that was in 1990 when she was on a train to London – she came up with the idea for Harry Potter during the journey. Rowling had no pen and – can you imagine that she was too shy to ask anyone for something to write with?

20 NAOMI: Oh, really?

JEFF: Actually, this was the best thing that could have happened because it gave her the full four hours on the train to think up the story.

NAOMI: Why did she choose the name "Potter" for her hero?

JEFF: That's a good question! J. K. used to play witch and wizard with Ian Potter,
25 her childhood neighbour.

NAOMI: Oh, I see. Jeff, you say J. K. Rowling. What do the letters "J. K." actually stand for?

JEFF: Joanne Kathleen. Rowling's first *Harry Potter* book was published under the simple name Joanne Rowling. But her publishers advised her not to use
30 her full first name.

NAOMI: Oh, why's that?

JEFF: They were afraid that boys might not want to read a book written by a woman. So to reach a bigger readership and for want of a name, Rowling just picked up her grandmother's name and became Joanne Kathleen.

35 NAOMI: Oh! Is it right that working on the Harry Potter books was not always easy for J. K. Rowling, especially at the beginning?

JEFF: Yes, the time she wrote the first book was quite hard. After her mother's death she went to Portugal to work as a language teacher. She hoped to finish the manuscript there but she didn't manage. When she returned to Brit-
40 ain, she was jobless. So, she used every free minute and hurried to the nearest café to write as much as she could.

NAOMI: In a café?

JEFF: Yep … Rowling wrote most of her first book in a coffee shop in Edinburgh. She liked the hustle and bustle of customers coming in, buying their
45 coffee and meeting friends. And she could see the 400-year-old "George

Heriot's School" which gave her the inspiration for Hogwarts, the famous
school for magic. And ... she didn't have to make her own coffee.

[NAOMI: Hahaha.]

JEFF: But let's get serious again ... Can you imagine that in the early days pub-
50   lishers sent her away because they weren't interested in a fantasy novel on
      witchcraft and wizardry?

NAOMI: Really?

JEFF: It took her more than a year to find a publisher before her final break-
      through.

55 NAOMI: What's the secret behind her success? Is it pure talent?

JEFF: Well, on the one hand imagination is important, of course. On the other
      hand having discipline and sticking to your goal is most relevant. I think it's
      a mixture of different talents.

NAOMI: What an interesting story! ... Thanks so much, Jeff.

Now listen to the interview again and check your answers.

---

1. c) ... have been translated into 60 languages.
   *Hinweis: "Her books have been sold more than 400 million times in over
   200 countries and 60 languages." (Z. 6–8)*

2. a) ... Rowling's childhood dream.
   Hinweis:"Writing novels was Rowling's childhood dream." (Z. 11/12)

3. ... train (journey)/journey.
   *Hinweis: "Well, that was in 1990 when she was on a train to London –
   she came up with the idea for Harry Potter during the journey." (Z. 16/17)*

4. ... (childhood) neighbour.
   *Hinweis:"J. K. used to play witch and wizard with Ian Potter, her child-
   hood neighbour." (Z. 24/25)*

5. a) ... a strategy to get more readers.
   *Hinweis: "So to reach a bigger readership and for want of a name, Row-
   ling just picked up her grandmother's name and became Joanne Kathleen."
   (Z. 33/34)*

6. b) ... suffered a family loss.
   Hinweis: "After her mother's death she went to Portugal ..." (Z. 37/38)

7. a) ... gave her the idea for Hogwarts.
   *Hinweis: " ... she could see the 400-year-old 'George Heriot's School'
   which gave her the inspiration for Hogwarts ..." (Z. 45/46)*

8. ... publishers ...

✎ **Hinweis:** *"It took her more than a year to find a publisher before her final breakthrough." (Z. 53/54)*

9. ... talents.

✎ **Hinweis:** *"I think it's a mixture of different talents." (Z. 57/58)*

2 Hörverstehen Teil 2: *English – a changing language*

> *Jared Warren and Kim Dakuma, two senior students at Woodpeck High, are doing a presentation on "English – a changing language" in class. First read the tasks of the quiz (1–9). Then listen to the presentation. Tick the correct box or complete the sentences while you are listening. Tick only **one** box. At the end you will hear the presentation again. Now read the tasks (1–9). You have 90 seconds to do this.*
> *Now listen to the presentation and do the tasks of the quiz.*

1 MRS BROWN: Quiet down everyone! ... Okay ... Jared and Kim are going to do their presentation now. While you're listening, you have to fill in a quiz. So listen carefully ...

JARED WARREN: Have you ever met a person who just keeps talking on and on
5 with no end in sight? If you have, you might have wondered if he or she would ever run out of words! But this won't happen, because the English language changes all the time. If you look back to old English – like a thousand years ago, English was very similar to German. Then you move on to, say, the time of the famous English poet William Shakespeare: early modern
10 English ... Yes, yes, I know, but he invented over 1,700 of our common words by changing nouns into verbs, changing verbs into adjectives, or connecting words which were never used together before. It's only when printing was invented around 1450 that the English language started to become standardised.

15 KIM DAKUMA: Yes, and today English is widespread. Did you know that English is the official language of 54 different countries and that there are 340 million people whose mother tongue is English? Together with the people who use English as a second language that makes one billion people worldwide. That means it's the most commonly spoken language across the globe.
20 Of course, there are other languages which are spoken by many people, like Chinese for example. But when we look at its use in different areas of education, science and research, English is the only global language.

JARED WARREN: That means English is used on the whole planet in many different fields. For example more than half of the world's technical and scientific magazines and books as well as three quarters of the world's mail are in English. In terms of pronunciation and construction English is used in a special way in more than 125 dialects worldwide.

It's very difficult to estimate the exact number of words in the English language. But there are supposed to be about 350,000 words altogether. A normally educated person knows about 20,000 words, but you only need about 850 words to be able to communicate in everyday life. And this might be interesting for our exchange student from Germany: after 4 years of learning English as a second language, students usually use about 8,000 words.

It seems like English will stay the most widely used language for some time; but it still changes every day. People play with it and sometimes the changes they make stay. They shorten words and sometimes they use letters to get their message across. Just think of our own text messages.

KIM DAKUMA: Interesting, isn't it? – But let's finish with some funny facts about the English language. Did you know that *stewardess* is the longest word that is typed with only the left hand? And when you tell somebody *goodbye* you really say *God be with you*, because that was its original meaning. And, for example, there are no words that rhyme with the words *month* and *angel*.

MRS BROWN: Great, thank you very much for your interesting presentation.

Now listen to the presentation again and check your answers.

Ende des Hörverstehenstests.

1. ... run out ...
   Hinweis: " ... *you might have wondered if he or she would ever run out of words! But this won't happen, because the English language changes all the time.*" (Z. 5–7)

2. c) ... was influenced by W. Shakespeare.
   Hinweis: "*Then you move on to, say, the time of the famous English poet William Shakespeare: early modern English.*" (Z. 8–10)

3. ... printing ...
   Hinweis: "*It's only when printing was invented around 1450 that the English language started to become standardised.*" (Z. 12–14)

4. b) ... by 340 million native speakers.
   ✏ *Hinweis:* " ... and that there are 340 million people whose mother tongue is English?" (Z. 16/17)

5. ... education ...
   ✏ *Hinweis:* "But when we look at its use in different areas of education, science and research, English is the only global language." (Z. 21/22)

6. b) ... 3/4 of postal communication.
   ✏ *Hinweis:* " ... as well as three quarters of the world's mail are in English." (Z. 25/26)

7. c) ... 8,000 words after 4 years of learning English.
   ✏ *Hinweis:* " ... after 4 years of learning English as a second language, students usually use about 8,000 words." (Z. 32/33)

8. ... shorten/play with ...
   ✏ *Hinweis:* "They shorten words and sometimes they use letters to get their message across." (Z. 36/37)

9. c) ... "goodbye" comes from the greeting "God be with you".
   ✏ *Hinweis:* "And when you tell somebody goodbye you really say God be with you, because that was its original meaning." (Z. 40/41)

3 Leseverstehen: *One world – different cultures? Festivals spreading around the world!*

1. b) ... turned Halloween into a commercial party.
   ✏ *Hinweis:* "Across the globe millions of people dress up in fancy costumes to celebrate 'All Hallow-Eves'! Unfortunately, only few know the idea and tradition behind it. Nowadays people only like to buy funny decorations, crazy costumes and lots of sweets." (Z. 3–6)

2. c) ... change cultural practices of the English-speaking world.
   ✏ *Hinweis:* "More and more British and American people join in festivals of immigrant culture that are not originally theirs." (Z. 9–11)

3. a) the victory of good over evil/the victory of knowledge over ignorance/the victory of light over darkness
   ✏ *Hinweis:* "Diwali means 'a row of lamps', which are lit to suggest the victory of good over evil, light over darkness and knowledge over ignorance." (Z. 13/14)

b) family values

   ✦ *Hinweis:* *"The festival also marks a new beginning of family values ..." (Z. 14/15)*

4. a) People from different cultural backgrounds come together.

   ✦ *Hinweis:* *"Since 2002 mass celebrations in Trafalgar Square have been held every year with English people coming from different cultural backgrounds." (Z. 20–22)*

   b) People meet and celebrate *Diwali* together./The celebrations are free and open to all.

   ✦ *Hinweis:* *"They meet and celebrate* Diwali *together with a colourful mix of music, dance, live performances, displays and food stalls. And what is important, too, the celebrations in Trafalgar Square are free and open to all." (Z. 22–25)*

5. b) ... celebrate a huge and peaceful festival.

   ✦ *Hinweis:* *"The idea for* 'Diwali *in Trafalgar Square' was born when three friends had a 'collective dream': a vision of a harmonious and grand mass celebration by London's multi-cultural community." (Z. 25–27)*

6. a) ... was given official status in 2007.

   ✦ *Hinweis:* *"Later, in 2007, the former president George W. Bush and the Congress of the United States officially recognized the religious and historical importance of* Diwali." (Z. 32–34)*

7. a) ... is a popular and crazy social event.

   ✦ *Hinweis:* *" ... a celebration of health, happiness, and individuality, bringing people from all races and ages together to create a five kilometre painting of colourful fun." (Z. 43–45)*

8. a) Athletes are powered in bright colours.

   ✦ *Hinweis:* *"Just like in the* Holi *celebration the athletes are powdered in bright colours ..." (Z. 45/46)*

   b) People collect money for social projects./People celebrate health, happiness and individuality.

   ✦ *Hinweis:* *" ... the organisation chooses a local charity in each city it visited, and has raised donations for over 60 local and national social projects ..." (Z. 48/49) / "... celebration of health, happiness, and individuality" (Z. 43/44)*

9. c) ... he welcomes the influence of different cultures.

   ✦ *Hinweis:* *Bei dieser Aufgabe lässt sich die Antwort nicht an einer einzelnen Textstelle festmachen, sondern ergibt sich aus dem Gesamtein-*

druck des Artikels. Der Autor bzw. die Autorin schildert den Einfluss von Festen und Bräuchen aus anderen Kulturen als durchwegs positiv, da das gemeinsame Feiern Menschen verschiedenster Herkunft miteinander in Kontakt bringt und verbindet. Sein/Ihr Fazit „What a <u>colourful</u> world we live in!" greift nicht nur das Bild der mit Farbpulver beworfenen Teilnehmer während des „Color Run" wieder auf, sondern drückt seine/ ihre Unterstützung für kulturelle Vielfalt aus.

10. 1. D
    2. F
    3. B
    4. E
    5. A
    6. C

Zweiter Prüfungsteil: Wortschatz – Schreiben

Miss Liberty

4. Wortschatz: *Teen advice*

1. mixed/different/contradictory/...

2. a) worried

3. b) conflict

4. rebel/fight/protest/...

5. feeling/attitude/opinion/...

6. a) copy
   behaviour/ways/conduct/style/...

7. d) solving

8. mistakes/decisions/...
   consequences/result/...

9. responsible/important/there ...

10. experience/attitude/knowledge ...

5 Schreiben

Hinweis: Bei den Schreibaufgaben gibt es keine konkreten Vorgaben, wie viele Wörter deine Antworten umfassen sollen. Um die volle Punktzahl zu bekommen, müssen jedoch unbedingt alle Aspekte, die in der Angabe genannt werden, in deiner Lösung vorkommen – d. h., deine Texte sollten auf keinen Fall zu kurz sein. Als grobe Richtlinie solltest du in Aufgabe 5.1 mindestens 80 Wörter, in 5.2 mindestens 100 Wörter und in 5.3 a bzw. 5.3 b mindestens 120 Wörter schreiben. Lies deine Lösungen noch einmal genau durch, wenn du fertig bist, um Flüchtigkeitsfehler zu vermeiden.

1. *Hinweis:* In dieser Aufgabe sollst du das Problem, mit dem die Erzählerin zu kämpfen hat, und ihren „unkonventionellen" Lösungsversuch in eigenen Worten zusammenfassen, d. h., das Grundthema des Textes kurz skizzieren.

In 1975 Monica's mother made a lot of money. She designed and sold toy puppets for the 200th birthday of the Statue of Liberty. She put the money into saving accounts and promised her children that they would get it when they were sixteen. Then they could do whatever they wanted with it.

Now that Monica is turning sixteen she wants to fulfil her dream and play the guitar on the Boulevard Saint Michel in Paris. But her mother refuses to keep her promise. Monica gets very angry and has a long and heated discussion with her mom.

Back in her room she sees the puppet of the Statue of Liberty and suddenly an idea comes to her mind. She decides to dress up as the Statue of Liberty and demonstrate for her "freedom" to go to Paris in the front garden.

142 words

2. *Hinweis:* Bei dieser Aufgabe geht es darum, die Gefühle sowohl von Monica selbst als auch von ihrer Mutter zu beschreiben und nachvollziehbar zu machen – du musst dich also in beide Sichtweisen hineinversetzen können.

Monica is very angry because her mother doesn't keep her promise. She has been looking forward to making music on the streets of Paris and is disappointed that her big dream won't come true. However, Monica does not give up without a fight and decides to protest against her mother's refusal.

Monica's mother, on the other hand, thinks that Monica's dream is a foolish idea. She doesn't want her daughter to go to Paris on her own because this would be too dangerous for a sixteen-year-old girl and she would be worried. Moreover, she says that she needs Monica at home during the summer to look after the twins.

109 words

3. a) *Hinweis:* Bei dieser Aufgabe musst du persönlich zu der Aussage Stellung nehmen, dass man sich immer an Versprechen halten soll. Sammle zunächst deine Ideen und mache dir Notizen. Wie in der Angabe gefordert, musst du in deiner Lösung sowohl Argumente für diese Sichtweise als auch Argumente dagegen anführen, d. h., du solltest überlegen, unter welchen Umständen Versprechen gebrochen werden können (oder sogar müssen). Versuche, beide Seiten sachlich gegeneinander abzuwägen. Deine Argumentation im Hauptteil solltest du durch einen (hinführenden) Einleitungssatz und einen (zusammenfassenden) Schlusssatz einrahmen.

Personally, I think the statement, "You should never break a promise", is a good guideline for most (but perhaps not all) situations.

On the one hand it is very important to keep a promise, because it builds up trust. You can count on each other that things will happen as promised. When somebody offers their help when you are in need, you must be able to rely on it. In this case friendships become even stronger.

On the other hand a promise is something you can't change anymore. Monica's mother promised her daughter that she could do anything she wanted with the money when she turned sixteen. She probably didn't think that she would be taken by her word several years later, but now Monica is understandably angry. Therefore, one should be very careful not to make promises one cannot keep.

Nevertheless, I think that there are situations where breaking a promise is allowed. Imagine, for example, that one of your classmates is bullied by older pupils, but asks you not to talk to anyone about it. In this case, you might have to tell your friend that you won't be able to keep the promise and that you will inform your parents, a teacher or even the police if he or she is in danger.

To conclude, I believe that keeping a promise is important, but that there are some exceptions. Monica's mother certainly made a big mistake when she said, "Sure, you bet."

245 words

b) *Hinweis:* Bei dieser Aufgabe kommt es darauf an, in deiner Lösung an den Stil der vorgegebenen Kurzgeschichte anzuknüpfen. Du solltest deinen Text daher in der Ich-Perspektive formulieren und das simple past als Erzählzeit verwenden. Versuche, dich in die Figuren hineinzuversetzen und überlege, wie du in der vorgegebenen Situation reagieren würdest. Um neben der Sichtweise der Ich-Erzählerin (Monica) auch die Reaktionen ihrer Mutter darzustellen, kannst du beim Schreiben zwischen Dialogen und erzählenden Passagen abwechseln.

"Are you hungry, Monica? I made a nice breakfast for you."

"Thank you, mom."

I smiled weakly and sat down in the kitchen. After my long night outside, a hot breakfast sounded like paradise.

"Mom, I need to talk to you. I was so furious yesterday, because you didn't keep your promise. I thought it was unfair that you wouldn't allow me to go to Paris."

"Oh, poor sweetheart. I made a mistake when I promised to let you go to Paris at the age of sixteen. The money I earned made me blind. I wasn't thinking of the consequences at that moment. You are only a teenager – going to Paris alone at your age is just too dangerous."

"But during the night I had an idea, Mommy. What about going to Paris with a youth organization?"

Mom began to smile and took me in her arms. "That sounds good. Yes, then I wouldn't be so worried anymore."

I gave her a kiss. "My friend Laura told me about an organization like that. I'll call her later and ask her if we can go together."

Mom was very relieved and said, "Auntie Dorothy wants to see us and I'll ask her if she can look after the other children while you're away. I'm sure she'll do it."

"Oh Mommy, I love you so much."

"Let's go to your father and tell him."

So after a day and night of arguing, both of us left the kitchen feeling very happy. *249 words*

Erster Prüfungsteil: Hörverstehen – Leseverstehen

1   Hörverstehen Teil 1: *Hockey – Canada's national sport*

CBC Radio runs a weekly program called Discover Canada. *The presenter, Angele Alain, talks to her guest Paul Kitchen.*

- *First read the tasks.*
- *Then listen to the interview.*
- *While you are listening, tick the correct box or fill in the information.*
- *At the end you will hear the interview again.*
- *Now read the tasks. You have **90 seconds** to do this.*
- *Now listen to the interview and do the tasks.*

---

1. Early ice-hockey …
   a) ☐   had no fixed rules.
   b) ☐   was invented in Canada.
   c) ☐   meant scoring a goal with a ball.

2. The first real ice-hockey match …
   a) ☐   had no break.
   b) ☐   took place outside.
   c) ☐   was an unexpected hit.

3. Watching early ice-hockey matches was dangerous. Why?
   Give **one** example.

   _____

4. Today's ice-hockey is different …
   a) ☐   thanks to better ice.
   b) ☐   because of bigger teams.
   c) ☐   except for the techniques.

5. Early ice-hockey equipment was very different from today's.
   Give **one** example.

   _____

6. In the 1st ice-hockey league match …
   a) ☐ the Montreal Canadians lost.
   b) ☐ the start of the game was very late.
   c) ☐ some team members "went on strike".

7. Canadians like ice-hockey very much. Why?
   a) _____

   b) _____

8. The majority of Canadians …
   a) ☐ watch all the matches on TV.
   b) ☐ have read a politician's hockey book.
   c) ☐ want their kids to learn how to skate.

2   Hörverstehen Teil 2: *Bad luck in English* by Jon Hassler 🔘

You are going to hear a story about Thomas who goes to see his teacher, Mr. Singleton, on the last day before the summer holidays.

> • *First read the tasks.*
> • *Then listen to the story.*
> • *While you are listening tick the correct box.*
> • *At the end you will hear the story again.*
> • *Now read the tasks. You have **90 seconds** to do this.*
> • *Now listen to the story and do the tasks.*

1. Thomas wants to talk to Mr. Singleton because …
   a) ☐ he wants a better grade.
   b) ☐ he wants to see his report card.
   c) ☐ his parents are angry with him.

2. Mr. Singleton …
   a) ☐ is busy and sends Thomas away.
   b) ☐ suggests talking about Thomas's grade.
   c) ☐ sees no possibility to change Thomas's grade.

3. Thomas …
   a) ☐ failed every test.
   b) ☐ feels unjustly treated.
   c) ☐ knows little about English.

4. Thomas's problem is that he …
   a) ☐ is lazy.
   b) ☐ pays no attention.
   c) ☐ is bored during classes.

5. At the beginning of term Thomas …
   a) ☐ had other priorities.
   b) ☐ was a model student.
   c) ☐ missed some classes.

6. The number 47 stands for …
   a) ☐ all the missed classes.
   b) ☐ the missing homework.
   c) ☐ all the tests Thomas failed.

7. Thomas …
   a) ☐ has a cruel father.
   b) ☐ needs his part-time job.
   c) ☐ tries to fool his teacher.

8. Thomas …
   a) ☐ can hand in a story.
   b) ☐ must improve his spelling.
   c) ☐ needs to change his attitude.

9. Thomas …
   a) ☐ is proud of himself.
   b) ☐ decides to play it cool.
   c) ☐ accepts the suggestion.

3 Leseverstehen

Another lost generation

Canadian Prime Minister
Stephen Harper apologizes to Canadian Indians

1 From the 1890s until 1996 over 150,000 young Canadian Indians were taken from their families and sent to residential schools to wipe out[1] their native languages and culture. Thomas Louttit, 66,
5 was one of these children. When he was 5 years old, he and his sister were taken from their home and put on a motorboat to a residential school in Fort George, a day's journey.

Thomas Louttit doesn't remember much of what he learned, but he is very
10 much aware of what he lost: "We were not allowed to speak our own language. We were taught in English or French, and we had to eat European food," he says. The parents of these Canadian Indian children weren't sure where their children spent ten months of the year, they didn't know that they had to do heavy work, were beaten and physically and sexually misused.

15 What Louttit's parents did not know either, was that their children had to answer to numbers. "They gave us a number. That's all our name was. One summer after I went home, my father was calling and calling me," Louttit recalls. "I didn't answer him because I was not used to hearing my name. He asked what was the matter with me. I never told him."

20 Indian schools were started in the late 19th century when the Canadian government believed that Indians could only survive in the modern world if they learned to live and think like white people. Over a century, Canada's government and churches built about 130 schools for young natives to "kill the Indian in the child", as a government official said in 1920.

25 Thousands of young Canadian-Indians were traumatized at school from the 1890s until 1996. They felt lonely and misunderstood and lost their culture and their self-respect. When these children grew up, they could not get jobs because they had been too sad at school to learn properly. Many of them started drinking and many committed suicide. Louttit suffered from alcoholism for years. He only
30 got better when he started living his own life again by going back to his roots and teaching Indian traditions to young people.

Outside Canada most people didn't know anything about all this. On June 11, 2008, the Canadian Prime Minister Stephen Harper formally apologized to Canada's First Nations[2]: "I stand before you to offer an apology to former students of
35 Indian residential schools. The treatment of children in these schools is a sad chapter in our history. [...] The government of Canada sincerely apologizes and asks the forgiveness of the aboriginal peoples of this country for failing them so profoundly[3]."

Many Canadian Indians are not sure about Harper's apology. Some believe
40 Harper was just trying to get more votes from Canada's Indian citizens. Mary
Simpson, president of the Inuit Tapiriit Kanatam[4], says that "forgiveness must be
earned. Our people are not going to accept the apology until the government has
done all it can to give them a chance to rebuild their broken lives." Thomas
Louttit, now a leader of the Moose Factory First Nation[5], feels the same way:
45 "It's not from him inside. Someone else wrote it for him."

On the other hand, Patrick Brazeau, chief of the *Congress of Aboriginal Peoples*, has called Harper's apology "the moral and right thing to do", and many
other Canadian Indians feel like him. However, it will be very difficult to satisfy
the proud First Nations who feel that the Europeans have stolen their honor. In
50 Louttit's words: "It's going to be a long journey."

*Text based on: Maggie Farley: Canada to apologize for abuse of native students. In: Los Angeles
Times, June 10, 2008. Parliament of Canada: 39th Parliament, 2nd Session, Edited Hansard
No. 110, June 11, 2008. Article "Canadian Indian residential school system" from Wikipedia,
the Free Encyclopedia, licensed under CC-BY-SA 3.0.*
Foto © Mike Carraccetto / Getty Images

1 to wipe out – to make something disappear
2 First Nations – the native people of Canada
3 to fail someone profoundly – to not give enough attention to somebody/not do right by somebody
4 Inuit Tapiriit Kanatam – Canada's national Inuit organization; the Inuit are one of the native
  people in Canada
5 Moose Factory First Nation – a large Indian tribe with more than 200,000 members living in
  Canada

- *First read the text.*
- *Then do the tasks 1–11.*
- *For tasks 1, 5, 9 and 10 tick the correct box.*
- *For tasks 2, 4, 7, 8 and 11 tick the correct box and quote from the text.*
- *For tasks 3 and 6 fill in the information.*

---

1. For several years many Canadian Indian children …
   a) ☐ were educated at home.
   b) ☐ had to go to special schools.
   c) ☐ learned their native language.

2. As an adult, Thomas Louttit feels that something was taken away from him.
   This statement is … ☐ true ☐ false … because the text says …

_____   _____

3. At the residential schools Canadian Indian children were forced to …
   a) _____
   b) _____

4. The families of the Canadian Indian children were informed about the education methods.
   This statement is … ☐ true ☐ false … because the text says …

   _____

5. The Canadian government wanted …
   a) ☐ to give Indians a religious education.
   b) ☐ the Indians to fit into European culture.
   c) ☐ to protect Indians from modern influence.

6. Residential schools had negative consequences for the Canadian Indians in their later lives. Give two examples.
   a) _____
   b) _____

7. Until today, Thomas Louttit still can't deal with his past.
   This statement is … ☐ true ☐ false … because the text says …

   _____

8. This part of Canadian history is little known world-wide.
   This statement is … ☐ true ☐ false … because the text says …

   _____

9. The Canadian Prime Minister …
   a) ☐ said sorry to the Canadian Indians.
   b) ☐ defended the government's policy.
   c) ☐ ignored the story of the residential schools.

10. The aboriginal people in Canada …
    a) ☐ want the government to do more.
    b) ☐ believe the Prime Minister was honest.
    c) ☐ think it's time to excuse the injustice and move on.

11. Canadian Indians need time to deal with their past.
    This statement is … ☐ true ☐ false … because the text says …

    _____

I'm sick of "checking in"!

4   Wortschatz: *Young people and parents*

The two bloggers Sherry and Brett blog about things that are important to young adults. Check their latest entry.

- *Fill in suitable words or tick the correct box.*

There are a lot of things young people and their parents fight about.

1.   Getting along with one's parents can sometimes be _____
     especially if we feel misunderstood or treated unfairly.

2.   That's why it is so important to work for a good _____
     with your parents.

3.   How does this work? – One of the golden rules is simply: when you have different opinions, keep _____. Don't get too excited!

4.   What's more, it is important for good parent-teen relationships to talk about
     the _____ that are troubling you.

5.   And be honest, parents won't be …
     a) ☐ upset   b) ☐ excited
     c) ☐ sentimental   d) ☐ serious
     if we talk and solve problems together.

6.   Nevertheless, we often feel under pressure to fulfil our parents'
     _____.

7.   Growing up means fighting for …
     a) ☐ profit.   b) ☐ independence.
     c) ☐ agreement.   d) ☐ practicality.

8.   But you can't always get what you want. Young people also need
     _____ they have to accept and live by.

9.   We must accept and learn that we are …
     a) ☐ controlled   b) ☐ sensible
     c) ☐ responsible   d) ☐ powerful
     for our actions.

10. And that means that we also need to see the …
    a) ☐ influences   b) ☐ reactions
    c) ☐ consequences   d) ☐ duties
    of our actions.

11. Life can really be …
    a) ☐ difficult   b) ☐ more complicated
    c) ☐ troublesome   d) ☐ easier
    if you remember these basic ideas.

12. To avoid trouble, it's sometimes necessary for every member of the family
    to _____.

13. And remember, it's no easy task for parents to …
    a) ☐ change   b) ☐ accept
    c) ☐ shape   d) ☐ develop
    that their children want to make their own decisions.

Sherry and Brett

5   Schreiben

I'm sick of "checking in"! by Brent Stephenson

1 My father and I disagreed about curfew[1]. He would say I had to be in by 22:30
  on weekdays, and by 00:30 on weekends. There were no exceptions without asking first. I told him, "I'm seventeen and shouldn't have to have a curfew." Then I
  reminded him that in less than a year I would be away at college. There I would
5 be coming in whenever I liked. He told me that what I did in college was my
  choice, but that while living at home, the rules stood. He said he thought the curfew was fair. If I wanted to stay out later, all I had to do was ask. I only had to
  give him an acceptable reason. I told him that it was like having to "check in" –
  which made me feel like a junior-high kid. I also told him that it was time he let
10 me be responsible for myself. To this he explained that while a curfew may
  sound like a restriction[2], it's really about people looking out for one another.
     We just went around and around on curfew, never seeing eye to eye on it[3].
     The next Friday after one pretty heated exchange, my dad and I had tickets to
  see our town's professional football league opening-day game. They were good
15 tickets, and it was the season's opening night, so we were really looking forward
  to going. On the day of the game, my dad had a really important out-of-town
  business meeting with some major clients he was meeting for the first time. He
  was driving to a nearby city to meet with these clients and informed me that the
  time between his getting home and our leaving for the game would be tight[4].

20   That afternoon I made sure we didn't have to waste one minute but could leave the second he walked in. I turned off the radio and the TV and necessary lights. I put the tickets in my jacket, and got the sports jacket from his closet I knew he would be wearing. I placed our jackets on the sofa next to the door. When a half-hour had passed from the time he said he would be home, I under-
25 stood that he was a little late.

    But then, nearly a whole hour passed. I was getting really irritated. I mean, we were going to miss the kick-off! And why hadn't he phoned me and let me know he was going to be really late? I had hurried through my homework. If I had known he would be late, I could have taken my time and been a little more thor-
30 ough. And if he had phoned maybe I would have found a ride to the game, and Dad could just meet me there. Anxiously pacing the floor[5], yet another half-hour passed. That's when my frustration turned to anger. How selfish of my father! Now we were going to miss the whole game! I would rather have had to sit alone at the game, instead of missing the whole thing!

35   When another half-hour passed, my anger turned to fear. What if something terrible had happened to my dad, like he had had a heart attack or had been in an accident, or something? I began to really worry. After all, I had already called his cell phone – about ten times – and there had been no answer. I called Mom (my parents are divorced) to see if she knew where my father was. But she hadn't
40 talked to my father for a few days and knew nothing of my father's schedule. So then I began calling some of my father's colleagues; none of them knew anything about where he could be. One didn't even know he had spent the day away from the office.

    I was so worried, thinking the worst had happened.

45   Finally, the phone rang, and my dad said breathlessly …

Text © Brent Stephenson: I'm sick of "checking in". In: Jennifer Youngs/Bettie B. Youngs (Ed.): Taste Berries for Teens 3. Deerfield Beach: Health Communications 2002, pp. 124-126.

1 curfew – a time when children must be home in the evening
2 restriction – a rule that limits what you can do
3 to see eye to eye on sth – here: to agree/to reach agreement
4 tight – here: difficult to manage/(a) short (time)
5 to pace the floor – to walk up and down, especially because you are feeling nervous or angry

1. **Describe** what you get to know about the young man and the rules he has to follow at home.

2. **Explain** the young man's opinion of the curfew and "checking in" and how he feels when his father is late one night.

3. You have a choice here. Choose **one** of the following tasks.

   a) *"Curfew is not an instrument to control or ruin your fun, it's a matter of responsibility."*
   Comment on the statement from **your** point of view.
   Include the following aspects:
   – Write about your own experience.
   – Give your personal opinion on the statement.
   – Give examples of situations where rules are (not) a matter of discussion.
   – Write a conclusion and state what rules are important for young adults.

   or

   b) *"Finally, the phone rang, and my dad said breathlessly ..."*
   Write a suitable ending in the way the story is told.
   Include the following aspects:
   – continue the telephone conversation
   – describe the father's and son's first contact after the telephone call
   – the father's and son's reactions to what had happened
   – the reasons for their behavior during the quarrel
   – the deal the father and his son make for the future

Lösungsvorschläge

Erster Prüfungsteil: Hörverstehen – Leseverstehen

Mittlerer Schulabschluss – Haupttermin

Wichtige Hinweise: Alle Texte, die im Folgenden zu hören sind, werden zweimal vorgespielt. Vor dem ersten Hören wird Zeit gegeben, sich mit den Aufgaben vertraut zu machen. Der Hörverstehenstest besteht aus zwei Teilen.

---

1 Hörverstehen Teil 1: *Hockey – Canada's national sport*

CBC Radio runs a weekly program called Discover Canada. *The presenter, Angele Alain, talks to her guest Paul Kitchen. First read the tasks. Then listen to the interview. While you are listening, tick the correct box or fill in the information. At the end you will hear the interview again. Now read the tasks.*
*You have **90 seconds** to do this.*
Now listen to the interview and do the tasks.

---

1 ANGELE ALAIN: Welcome to *Discover Canada*. With me in the studio today is ice-hockey expert Paul Kitchen. Hi Paul, thanks for coming.

PAUL KITCHEN: My pleasure.

ANGELE ALAIN: Paul, tell us, when did people start playing ice-hockey?

5 PAUL KITCHEN: Well, forms of the game have been played for centuries in all northern countries, not just here in Canada. Not regular hockey with rules or anything, it was just unorganized fun. The idea was always similar: people getting out on the ice with their skates on, trying to push a ball or a piece of wood around with a stick.

10 ANGELE ALAIN: Mmh, well, what about the first real ice-hockey match?

PAUL KITCHEN: Well, ... there were nine players on each team. They played in an indoor arena with natural ice. The match had two 30-minute-periods and about 40 people came to watch it. That was a huge success because it was something new.

15 ANGELE ALAIN: Okay ...

PAUL KITCHEN: The only trouble was that there was no fence which separated the players from the spectators and the goals had no nets. So for safety reasons the players tried to get a flat piece of wood into the other team's goal. Before that players had used balls which often flew into the audience and hit

20 people.

ANGELE ALAIN: Ugh, ouch! Paul, how has hockey developed over the years?

2015-11

PAUL KITCHEN: Well, a lot of things have changed. Erm, for a start the techniques of the players have improved a lot. It's a huge advantage that they don't play on natural ice anymore. Artificial ice is usually harder than natural ice. Then, for example, the number of players has been reduced to six per side.

ANGELE ALAIN: What about the equipment?

PAUL KITCHEN: Early skates were pretty simple. The skate was separate and fixed to the shoes or boots you were wearing. The players didn't wear helmets or have shoulder protection. Also, the sticks have changed a lot: there are still wooden sticks, but many professional league players also use sticks made from aluminum or fiberglass.

ANGELE ALAIN: I see. Today ice-hockey is played professionally. When was today's ice-hockey league formed?

PAUL KITCHEN: That was in 1917. In the first league game the Montreal Canadians played the Ottawa Senators. It wasn't a good day for the Ottawa Senators. Two of their players refused to come out on the ice at the start of the game because they thought their contracts and their pay were unfair. Halfway through the game however they finally showed up ... but it was too late. The Senators lost 7 : 4.

ANGELE ALAIN: Too bad! Paul, why do you think Canadians love ice-hockey so much?

PAUL KITCHEN: Well, first of all we are very proud of being the country that invented and developed the game. It was us who gave it to the world. Secondly it's a very tough sport. A lot of Canadians like to think of themselves as tough.

ANGELE ALAIN: Aha. So hockey is an important part of the Canadian identity? Is that right?

PAUL KITCHEN: Oh yes! Surveys show that 92 percent of Canadians believe every child should be able to skate. No wonder then that the hockey final of the last Olympic Games was watched by 80 percent of all Canadians.

ANGELE ALAIN: 80 percent?

PAUL KITCHEN: Mhm. And our Prime Minister wrote a book in 2013. Guess about what? Not about politics ... about ice-hockey!

ANGELE ALAIN: Interesting, Paul thank you very much for the moment. We'll be back with more fascinating information on Canada's most popular sport ...

Now listen to the interview again and check your answers.

1. a) … had no fixed rules.

   Hinweis: "*Not regular hockey with rules or anything, it was just unorganized fun.*" *(Z. 6/7)*

2. c) … was an unexpected hit.

   Hinweis: "*That was a huge success because it was something new.*" *(Z. 13/14)*

3. (there was) no fence/(there were) no goal nets/balls flew into the audience/balls hit people

   Hinweis: "*The only trouble was that there was no fence which separated the players from the spectators and the goals had no nets.*" *(Z. 16/17)* / "*Before that players had used balls which often flew into the audience and hit people.*" *(Z. 19/20)*

4. a) … thanks to better ice.

   Hinweis: "*It's a huge advantage that they don't play on natural ice anymore.*" *(Z. 23/24)*

5. simple skates/skate separate/skate fixed to shoes or boots/no helmets/no shoulder protection/sticks made from aluminum or fiberglass

   Hinweis: "*Early skates were pretty simple. The skate was separate and fixed to the shoes or boots you were wearing. The players didn't wear helmets or have shoulder protection. Also, the sticks have changed a lot: there are still wooden sticks, but many professional league players also use sticks made from aluminum or fiberglass.*" *(Z. 28–32)*

6. c) … some team members "went on strike".

   Hinweis: "*Two of their players refused to come out on the ice at the start of the game because they thought their contracts and their pay were unfair.*" *(Z. 37/38)*

7. a) (they are proud) they invented/developed the game/gave it to the world

   Hinweis: "*Well, first of all we are very proud of being the country that invented and developed the game. It was us who gave it to the world.*" *(Z. 43/44)*

   b) (it's a) tough sport

   Hinweis: "*Secondly it's a very tough sport. A lot of Canadians like to think of themselves as tough.*" *(Z. 44/45)*

8. c) … want their kids to learn how to skate.

   Hinweis: "*Surveys show that 92 percent of Canadians believe every child should be able to skate.*" *(Z. 48/49)*

2 Hörverstehen Teil 2: *Bad luck in English* by Jon Hassler

*You are going to hear a story about Thomas who goes to see his teacher, Mr. Singleton, on the last day before the summer holidays. First read the tasks. Then listen to the story. While you are listening tick the correct box. At the end you will hear the story again. Now read the tasks. You have **90 seconds** to do this. Now listen to the story and do the tasks.*

1　It all started in June, on the last day of school. Shocked, I was staring at my report card. I had an F in English. F – the worst of all grades! My parents would go crazy. That's why I decided to see Mr. Singleton. I thought I might convince him to change my grade.

5　　I went to Mr. Singleton's room. I found him sitting behind his desk.

"Thomas," he said, "I know why you are here. You are not satisfied with your grade."

"I'm in a state of shock," I said.

"All is not lost, Thomas. Sit down. Let's talk: nothing is hopeless." That
10　sounded like I had a chance.

"That's good to hear," I said. I sat down. Mr. Singleton smiled at me. "Mr. Singleton," I said, "I deserve better than an F in English. I did great on all your tests. I know everything you teach. And still, you're going to fail me. That's unfair!"

His smile faded.

15　"Unfair you say?" He looked at me. "Now, … it is true that you know a great deal about what I teach, but you have one great weakness: you do not work hard enough, young man."

"Not hard enough?"

"Exactly. Working hard enough means handing in written homework. Would
20　you care to tell me the number of written tasks you failed to hand in during the year?"

"Well, … I know I left out a few. But I had a job, Mr. Singleton. I couldn't always find time to do the tasks."

Mr. Singleton opened his grade book.

25　I had decided early in the year that I wouldn't trouble myself with English tasks. Doing written work just takes up too much of your free time. I thought I could get at least a C by simply showing up for class.

"Look at this," Mr. Singleton said pointing to my name in his grade book. Except for the few A's and B's I got on tests, all the other little squares after my
30　name were empty. Forty-seven blank squares.

"Those A's and B's don't make an F," I said.

"Those forty-seven empty squares stand for forty-seven F's. Even if there are a few A's and B's from your tests, it's still a very low average."

I decided to change my strategy and play on his sympathy – even tell a lie or
35 two … I told him my father would beat me black and blue. I also told him I would
lose my job at the pet store. I told him it might even kill my mother!

That's when he gave me a big horrible smile and I realized I had no chance.

"Thomas, I have a plan. That F can be changed to a B – if you write one long
story in a good style and free of mistakes. If you bring it to me on the first day of
40 school after the summer holidays I will change your grade."

"But in the summer I work full time in the pet store. I'm not sure I'd have the
time to work on English."

"If you wish to pass the course you will find the time. It is your one chance."

"Well, maybe I can work it out. Just tell a story in writing – is that it?"

45 "Yes. A story of some length."

"What length?"

He smiled and said, "Forty-seven pages."

Text © Jon Hassler: Four miles to Pinecone. New York: Fawcett Books 1977.

Now listen to the story again and check your answers.

Ende des Hörverstehenstests.

1. a) … he wants a better grade.
   *✎ **Hinweis:** "That's why I decided to see Mr. Singleton. I thought I might convince him to change my grade." (Z. 3/4)*

2. b) … suggests talking about Thomas's grade.
   *✎ **Hinweis:** "'All is not lost, Thomas. Sit down. Let's talk: nothing is hopeless.'" (Z. 9)*

3. b) … feels unjustly treated.
   *✎ **Hinweis:** "'Mr. Singleton,' I said, 'I deserve better than an F in English. I did great on all your tests. I know everything you teach. And still, you're going to fail me. That's unfair!'" (Z. 11–13)*

4. a) … is lazy.
   *✎ **Hinweis:** "'… you have one great weakness: you do not work hard enough, young man.'" (Z. 16/17)*

5. a) … had other priorities.
   *✎ **Hinweis:** "I had decided early in the year that I wouldn't trouble myself with English tasks. Doing written work just takes up too much of your free time." (Z. 25/26)*

6. b) ... the missing homework.
   Hinweis: "*Except for the few A's and B's I got on tests, all the other little squares after my name were empty. Forty-seven blank squares.*" *(Z. 29/30)*

7. c) ... tries to fool his teacher.
   Hinweis: "*I decided to change my strategy and play on his sympathy – even tell a lie or two ...*" *(Z. 34/35)*

8. a) ... can hand in a story.
   Hinweis: "*'Thomas, I have a plan. That F can be changed to a B – if you write one long story in a good style and free of mistakes. If you bring it to me on the first day of school after the summer holidays I will change your grade.'*" *(Z. 38–40)*

9. c) ... accepts the suggestion.
   Hinweis: "*'Well, maybe I can work it out. Just tell a story in writing – is that it?'*" *(Z. 44)*

3 Leseverstehen: *Another lost generation*

1. b) ... had to go to special schools.
   Hinweis: "*From the 1890s until 1996 over 150,000 young Canadian Indians were taken from their families and sent to residential schools to wipe out their native languages and culture.*" *(Z. 1–4)*

2. true
   "Thomas Louttit ... is very much aware of what he lost ..."
   Hinweis: Z. 9/10

3. a) speak only French or English / eat European food
   Hinweis: "*'We were not allowed to speak our own language. We were taught in English or French, and we had to eat European food,' he says.*" *(Z. 10/11)*

   b) do heavy work / answer to numbers
   Hinweis: "*The parents ... weren't sure where their children spent ten months of the year, they didn't know that they had to do heavy work ...*" *(Z. 12/13)* / "*What Louttit's parents did not know either, was that their children had to answer to numbers.*" *(Z. 15/16)*

4. false
   "The parents ... weren't sure where their children spent ten months of the year, they didn't know that they had to do heavy work ..." /

"What Louttit's parents did not know either, was that their children had to answer to numbers."
Hinweis: Z. 12–16

5. b) … the Indians to fit into European culture.
    Hinweis: "Indian schools were started in the late 19th century when the Canadian government believed that Indians could only survive in the modern world if they learned to live and think like white people." (Z. 20–22)

6. a) unemployment/(many Canadian Indians) could not get jobs/ low education
    Hinweis: "When these children grew up, they could not get jobs because they had been too sad at school to learn properly." (Z. 27/28)

    b) alcoholism/(many Canadian Indians started) drinking/(many Canadian Indians committed) suicide
    Hinweis: "Many of them started drinking and many committed suicide." (Z. 28/29)

7. false
    "He only got better when he started living his own life again by going back to his roots and teaching Indian traditions to young people."
    Hinweis: Z. 29–31

8. true
    "Outside Canada most people didn't know anything about all this."
    Hinweis: Z. 32

9. a) … said sorry to the Canadian Indians.
    Hinweis: "On June 11, 2008, the Canadian Prime Minister Stephen Harper formally apologized to Canada's First Nations …" (Z. 32–34)

10. a) … want the government to do more.
    Hinweis: "… 'forgiveness must be earned. Our people are not going to accept the apology until the government has done all it can to give them a chance to rebuild their broken lives.'" (Z. 41–43)

11. true
    "However, it will be very difficult to satisfy the proud First Nations who feel that the Europeans have stolen their honor. In Louttit's words: 'It's going to be a long journey.'"
    Hinweis: Z. 48–50

I'm sick of "checking in"!

4 Wortschatz: *Young people and parents*

1. difficult/hard/a problem/tough/stressful/…

2. relationship/…

3. calm/cool/…

4. problems/things/…

5. a) … upset …

6. expectations/demands/dreams/wishes/ideals/…

7. b) … independence.

8. rules/limits/limitations/…

9. c) … responsible …

10. c) … consequences …

11. d) … easier …

12. give in/make compromises/adapt/cooperate/…

13. b) … accept …

5 Schreiben

🖊 **Hinweis:** *Bei den Schreibaufgaben finden sich keine Vorgaben, wie viele Wörter deine Lösung umfassen soll. Als grobe Richtline solltest du bei Aufgabe 1 mindestens 80 Wörter, bei Aufgabe 2 mindestens 100 Wörter und bei Aufgabe 3 mindestens 120 Wörter schreiben.*
Achte darauf, dass in deiner Lösung wirklich alle Aspekte der Aufgabenstellung enthalten sind. Gehe deinen Text noch einmal durch und hake in Gedanken die einzelnen Elemente ab. Ganz zum Schluss solltest du deine Lösung noch einmal auf sprachliche Fehler hin kontrollieren – so vermeidest du, dass dir Punkte abgezogen werden.

1. *Hinweis: Bei dieser Aufgabe sollst du zum einen zusammenfassen, was du über den Jungen erfährst (Alter, Schule usw.). Zum anderen sollst du die Regeln, die der Junge zu Hause beachten muss, beschreiben. Lies den Text gut durch und markiere die entsprechenden Stellen oder mache dir Notizen.*

The young man in the story is seventeen years old and lives with his father because his parents are divorced. He is in his last year at school and will leave for college in less than a year. We also know that he and his father are fans of the local football team. They are both looking forward to going to the first match of the season.
The young man's father has set a curfew. The narrator has to be in by 22:30 on weekdays, and 00:30 on weekends. Exceptions are made only when he asks his father beforehand whether he is allowed to stay out later, and only if he gives an acceptable reason. *115 words*

2. *Hinweis: Hier musst du kurz darstellen, was der Junge von den Ausgangsregeln seines Vaters hält. Darüber hinaus sollst du erklären, wie sich der Junge fühlt, als sein Vater nicht rechtzeitig nach Hause kommt. Am besten gehst du den Text noch einmal Schritt für Schritt durch und machst dir Notizen oder markierst wichtige Stellen, bevor du deine Lösung ausformulierst.*

The young man is not happy about the curfew at all. He wants to be accepted as a grown-up and be responsible for himself – however, having to "check in" makes him feel like a small child. Although he and his father keep discussing the topic, they never really reach an agreement.
When his father is late one night, the young man doesn't mind too much at first. However, after an hour of waiting he gets more and more angry – why can't his father at least phone him? After another hour, he starts worrying, fearing that something terrible might have happened to his father because he can't reach him on his cell phone. The two seem to have changed roles as the son is at home now and worried, and the father is late without notifying the son. *137 words*

3. a) *Hinweis: Bei dieser Aufgabe sollst du zu der Aussage Stellung nehmen, dass eine Ausgangssperre kein Instrument der Kontrolle sei, sondern vielmehr eine Sache der Verantwortung. Mache dir zunächst Notizen und versuche dann, deine Lösung sinnvoll zu strukturieren. Gehe als erstes auf deine persönlichen Erfahrungen ein. Danach beschreibst du deine eigene Meinung zur vorgegebenen Aussage und nennst Beispiele, wann Regeln bzw. welche Regeln für dich besonders (oder nicht besonders) wichtig sind. Zum Schluss rundest du deinen Aufsatz ab, indem du noch einmal auf die Bedeutung von Regeln für junge Erwachsene zu sprechen kommst.*

Many parents set curfews that state what time their children have to be home at night. However, this often leads to conflict within the family: the parents want safety, the kids want freedom.

I once had a similar argument with my parents, who expected me to be home by 11:00 p.m., but I came back at 1:00 a.m. without phoning them. My mom and dad were still awake, started quarrelling with me, and told me that I was not allowed to go out for the following two weeks. At first, I was angry with them for being so strict, but then I realized that they had been really worried. I apologized and promised to at least phone them whenever I might be late.

Of course, I am not always happy when I have to leave a party before midnight. However, I understand that parents are concerned about the well-being of their children and that there are certain rules that we, as young people, should respect. This does not just concern curfew, but other rules as well, e. g. that minors should not consume alcohol, or smoke cigarettes. In the end, I believe the question of rules has a lot to do with respect. Parents should accept that their children need to develop independence and responsibility, and young adults should respect their parents' wish to protect them. *226 words*

b) ✏ *Hinweis: Bei dieser Aufgabe sollst du die Geschichte weiterführen. Hier darfst du kreativ sein – allerdings mit gewissen Einschränkungen. Zum einen musst du die fünf verschiedenen Aspekte, die in der Aufgabenstellung genannt werden, berücksichtigen. Zum anderen sollte sich deine Fortsetzung inhaltlich und stilistisch möglichst nahtlos an den ersten Teil der Geschichte anschließen. Du musst in deiner Antwort also auf die vorangegangene Handlung Bezug nehmen und (wegen des Telefonats, das Vater und Sohn führen) einige Dialogsequenzen einbauen. Die anderen, erzählten Passagen sollten (wie im ersten Teil der Geschichte) in der Ich-Perspektive und im* past tense *geschrieben sein.*

Finally, the phone rang, and my dad said breathlessly ...
"I'm so terribly sorry ... As you know I had a meeting with our new clients. Well, I didn't know that they wanted to invite me to dinner after our appointment, and as the business deal is really important for our company, I couldn't say no ..."
"You could have at least called," I replied, again full of anger.
"I know ... but it all happened so quickly. We went directly from the office to the restaurant, talking all the time. I didn't want to be impolite."
"I was really worried about you, and of course we also missed the match ..."

When my dad finally arrived home, looking tired and sad, I was no longer angry. "I'm just glad you're home and that nothing terrible happened," I finally said. "I guess I understand now what you went through when I came home late and didn't call." He gave me a hug.

"And I realized how easy it is to forget to call when you're in the middle of something else," he said.

"Well, maybe we should both try to stick to the rules in the future – no matter what we are up to, there should always be enough time for a quick phone call."

"You're absolutely right, son. I promise it won't happen again."

"Great. Then how about watching the match on TV?" I suggested.

"They're showing the replay now." So we both got some chips, went into the living room, and settled onto the couch.   *247 words*

Erster Prüfungsteil: Hörverstehen – Leseverstehen

1 Hörverstehen Teil 1: *Racing to help*

Together with her guest Dr. Michael Ryan, Mae Holland of CBC Radio Canada is presenting a historical race with a hero called Balto.

- *First read the tasks.*
- *Then listen to the interview.*
- *While you are listening, tick the correct box **or** write down the information needed.*
- *At the end you will hear the interview again.*
- *Now read the tasks. You have **90 seconds** to do this.*
- *Now listen to the interview and do the tasks.*

---

1. A town was highly alarmed because of …
    a) ☐ a serious illness.
    b) ☐ unexplained deaths.
    c) ☐ a medical substance.

2. The trouble was that …
    a) ☐ the pilot was ill.
    b) ☐ flights were too dangerous.
    c) ☐ the only plane was far away.

3. The solution was to …
    a) ☐ go on horseback.
    b) ☐ use the railroad.
    c) ☐ send sleighdogs.

4. Balto became a hero …
    a) ☐ to everybody's surprise.
    b) ☐ thanks to his leadership experience.
    c) ☐ because he had the most risky route.

5. During their journey the team faced life-threatening situations. Name **two**.
    a) _____
    b) _____

6. The team nearly failed when …
   a) ☐ Kaasen wanted to give up.
   b) ☐ they almost lost the serum.
   c) ☐ the wind damaged their equipment.

7. Balto enjoyed immediate fame and …
   a) ☐ had a good life.
   b) ☐ got a medal for bravery.
   c) ☐ was invited to New York.

After listening to the **whole** radio feature, complete this task.

8. Balto's story is that of …
   a) ☐ a tragic mission.
   b) ☐ a test of life and love.
   c) ☐ a challenge against time.

2 Hörverstehen Teil 2: *Easy money* by Gemma Ingram 🔊

You are going to hear a story about Stephanie who is worried about her grand-mother.

- *First read the tasks.*
- *Then listen to the story.*
- *While you are listening, tick the correct box **or** write down the information needed.*
- *At the end you will hear the story again.*
- *Now read the tasks. You have **90 seconds** to do this.*
- *Now listen to the story and do the tasks.*

---

1. Stephanie's granny likes modern technology …
   a) ☐ but mixes things up.
   b) ☐ and deals with it easily.
   c) ☐ and can work it with help.

2. Stephanie is surprised because her granny …
   a) ☐ managed the TV all alone.
   b) ☐ is enjoying an "old" TV broadcast.
   c) ☐ has successfully recorded a film.

3. Stephanie starts to worry …
   a) ☐ and questions the stranger's honesty.
   b) ☐ but cannot check on her granny daily.
   c) ☐ despite the new neighbour's nice looks.

4. Talking to Simon, Stephanie …
   a) ☐ calms down.
   b) ☐ makes a decision.
   c) ☐ sees her worries confirmed.

5. Stephanie's fears grow for several reasons. Give **two**.
   a) _____
   b) _____

6. Stephanie's worries turn out to be unnecessary. Why?
   _____

7. In the story "easy money" means that …
   a) ☐ Stephanie invested her money cleverly.
   b) ☐ granny earned money and got cheap help.
   c) ☐ the stranger profited from a person in need.

3   Leseverstehen

Harriet Tubman – Secret Agent

1 Harriet Tubman is considered to be the "Moses" of our people. Born a slave, she became famous for risking her life as a "conductor" on the Underground Railroad, a secret network of people who helped runaway slaves to
5 get to freedom in the northern United States and in Canada. In 1849 Harriet fled slavery to escape and live in Canada. Despite a reward on her head, she returned to the South at least 19 times to lead her family and hundreds of other slaves to freedom via the Underground
10 Railroad.

On more than one trip Harriet and her passengers had many close calls. But she always succeeded because she was a clever and very tough leader. She did what she could to trick people. Harriet often took slaves away on a Saturday night.
15 Most slaves did not have to work on Sundays. So their owners wouldn't miss them and start searching until Monday. Sometimes Harriet would hide her "passengers", then check to see if it was safe for them to come out or rest at a "station" on the way. Sometimes she poured pepper on the trail to confuse the dogs of the slave hunters or walk through water to hide their scent. Sometimes she didn't head
20 north right away. She hid her passengers near home until their owners thought they were long gone and stopped looking. One thing kept her safe: the pistol on her belt. She would not hesitate to use it in self-defense, but it was also a symbol to instruct slaves, making it clear that "dead Negroes tell no tales".

Harriet Tubman was very proud because she "never lost one passenger." Her
25 resistance towards slavery did not break with the outbreak of the Civil War[1]. During a time when women were usually restricted to traditional roles, she did her fair share of those jobs. For more than three years she nursed the sick and wounded. She became the first woman in American history to lead several expeditions into rebel territory, collecting information. Tubman was a short woman
30 without special features who moved unnoticed through rebel territory. This made her extremely useful as a scout and spy. Armed with knowledge of the location of cotton warehouses, ammunition depots, and slaves waiting to be liberated, Harriet thus made several military raids possible.

After the war, Harriet continued to help blacks create new lives in freedom.
35 But Harriet was poor and deeply in debt. She had spent her whole life helping others. After the war the U. S. government wouldn't give her money for her work during the war. She still owed money to a bank which threatened to take her house if she did not pay the money back.

A writer named Sarah Bradford heard about Harriet's problem and wanted to
40 help her. Harriet agreed to let Sarah write a book about her life. The book told
the amazing story of Harriet's escape from slavery and her work on the Underground Railroad. The book was very popular, and Bradford shared the money
she made from it with Harriet. This income helped pay Harriet's debts and saved
the Tubman house.

45 Harriet continued to help elderly black people. She took many who were old,
sick, and poor into the Harriet Tubman Home for the Elderly and cared for them
until she became too old and sick to care for herself. In 1911 she moved to that
same home next door. She died in 1913 from pneumonia[2]. Tubman must have
been between 88 and 98 years. She was buried in Auburn, New York, with full
50 military honors.

Harriet Tubman changed – and probably saved – the lives of hundreds of
African Americans by leading them out of slavery to freedom. Her courage, bravery, and dedication inspired many people during her time. And her life continues
to inspire people today.

© Thomas B. Allen: Harriet Tubman. Secret agent. How daring slaves and free Blacks spied for the Union during the Civil War. Washington, D.C.: National Geographic Children's Books 2006, pp. 9 f.

1 Civil War – the war fought in the US between the northern and the southern states from
  1861 to 1865
2 pneumonia – an illness of the lungs

- *Tick the correct box **and** support your answer by quoting from the text.*

---

1. A "conductor" was a person who …
   a) ☐ ran an anti-slavery movement.
   b) ☐ guided runaway slaves to liberty.
   c) ☐ drove the train that slaves boarded to flee.
   … because the text says …

---

2. Harriet Tubman was in danger many times.
   This statement is … ☐ true   ☐ false   … because the text says …

---

3. Harriet Tubman was good at helping slaves because she …
   a) ☐ was a creative thinker.
   b) ☐ kept to a certain routine.
   c) ☐ would have a break when tired.
   … because the text says …

4. Harriet Tubman was prepared to kill a slave to keep safe.
   This statement is …   ☐ true   ☐ false   … because the text says …

5. Harriet Tubman refused to behave like women were expected to at that time.
   This statement is …   ☐ true   ☐ false   … because the text says …

6. Harriet Tubman was a perfect spy …
   a) ☐ but was badly paid for the job.
   b) ☐ because she did not raise any suspicion.
   c) ☐ and was able to destroy valuable enemy supplies.
   … because the text says …

7. After the war, Harriet Tubman's support for ex-slaves carried on.
   This statement is …   ☐ true   ☐ false   … because the text says …

8. Harriet's money problems were solved …
   a) ☐ thanks to a profitable deal.
   b) ☐ when Harriet wrote her autobiography.
   c) ☐ because Sarah Bradford lent her money.
   … because the text says …

9. What we know for sure today is …
   a) ☐ the age Harriet Tubman reached.
   b) ☐ the cause of Harriet Tubman's death.
   c) ☐ the number of people Harriet Tubman helped.
   … because the text says …

This could happen to you

4   Wortschatz: *CyberSafety 101: Tactics for teens and young adults*

CyberSafety 101 has developed important guidelines for secure internet behavior.

> • *Fill in suitable words or tick the correct box.*

1. **Be careful when you shop online.** You can _____ a lot of money when buying books and other school supplies online.

2. But when it comes to giving out your financial information, only ...
   a) ☐ trust　　　　　b) ☐ believe in
   c) ☐ ask for　　　　d) ☐ phone up
   companies you know.

3. Before you click the "buy button", always _____ the seller and the payment details.

4. **Work securely from wireless networks.** Today's world means you can access the Internet from a variety of public locations. But open networks present ...
   a) ☐ an increased　　b) ☐ a difficult
   c) ☐ a popular　　　d) ☐ an admirable
   security risk.

5. If possible, you should _____ networks that have a network security key, which means information sent over them is encoded.

6. **Navigate social networking sites with care.** Social networking makes _____ with friends and sharing information easier than ever.

7. But they also open you up to a variety of online threats. So you need to be ...
   a) ☐ safe　　　　　b) ☐ careful
   c) ☐ secure　　　　d) ☐ aware
   when logging into online hotspots.

8. **Be watchful when sharing your PC.** You should not _____ your computer to friends and peers, but if you do, make sure they are operating under a limited-user account.

9. This will …
   a) ☐ turn down   b) ☐ shorten
   c) ☐ reduce   d) ☐ close
   the risk of viruses.

10. **Create** _____ **passwords and change them regularly.**
   Passwords help protect your computer and your various accounts from unauthorized access.

11. **Backup your data regularly.** Prepare yourself for worst case scenarios
   (your laptop crashing the night before a term paper is due) in order to …
   a) ☐ exclude   b) ☐ save
   c) ☐ stop   d) ☐ prevent
   a complete disaster. All you need to do is save critical information.

12. **Try to** _____ **the information you give out online.**
   Don't post too much information about yourself.

13. a) ☐ Developing …   b) ☐ Breaking …
    c) ☐ Stealing …   d) ☐ Destroying …
    identities is a real and growing problem.

So, be proactive in keeping your PC safe and secure.

5 Schreiben

This could happen to you author unknown

1 Shannon could hear the footsteps behind her as she walked toward home. The thought of being followed made her heart beat faster. She was afraid to look back and she was glad she was almost home.

To be safe she walked faster, didn't look back and reached home immediately.

5 Once inside, she leaned against the door for a moment, relieved to be in the safety of her home. After tossing her books on the sofa she decided to grab a snack and get online. There she could talk to strangers without being afraid. After all, no one knew who she really was and couldn't hurt her.

She logged on under her screen name ByAngel213. She checked her Buddy
10 List and saw GoTo123 was on. She sent him an instant message:

ByAngel213:	Hi. I'm glad you are on! I thought someone was following me home today.
GoTo123:	LOL You watch too much TV. Don't you live in a safe neighborhood?
ByAngel213:	Of course I do. LOL I guess it was my imagination.
GoTo123:	Unless you have given your name out on-line. You haven't done that have you?
ByAngel213:	Of course not. I'm not stupid you know.
GoTo123:	Did you have a softball game after school today?
ByAngel213:	Yes and we won!!
GoTo123:	That's great! Who did you play?
ByAngel213:	We played the Hornets. LOL Their uniforms are so gross! They look like bees. LOL
GoTo123:	What is your team called?
ByAngel213:	We are the Canton Cats. We have tiger paws on our uniforms. They are really cool.
GoTo123:	Did you pitch?
ByAngel213:	No. I play second base. I got to go. My homework has to be done before my parents get home. I don't want them mad at me. Bye!
GoTo123:	Catch you later. Bye.

Without much hesitation, GoTo123 went to the member menu and began to search for her profile. When it came up, he highlighted it and printed it out. He
35 took out a pen and began to write down what he knew about Angel so far.

He knew her name, birthday, age and her hobbies.

He knew she stayed by herself until 6:30 p.m. every afternoon until her parents came home from work. He knew she played softball on Thursday afternoons on the school team, and the team was named the Canton Cats. Her favorite num-
40 ber 7 was printed on her jersey. He knew she was in the eighth grade at the Canton Junior High School. She had told him all this in the conversations they had

had online.

GoTo123 decided it was time to teach Angel a lesson. One she would never forget.

45 Shannon didn't tell her parents about the incident[1] on the way home from the ballpark that day. She didn't want them to make a scene. Parents were always overreacting and hers were the worst. By Thursday, Shannon had forgotten about the footsteps following her.

Her game was in full swing when suddenly she felt someone staring at her. It 50 was then that the memory came back. She saw a man watching her closely. He smiled when she looked at him. He didn't look scary and she quickly forgot the sudden fear she had felt.

After the game, he sat on a bench while she talked to the coach. She noticed his smile once again as she walked past him. He nodded and she smiled back. He 55 noticed her name on the back of her shirt. Now he had to wait until it was time to make his move.

Shannon was in her room later that evening when she heard voices in the living room.

"Shannon, come here," her father called. He sounded upset and she couldn't 60 imagine why. She went into the room to see the man from the ballpark sitting on the sofa.

"Sit down," her father began. "This man has just told us a most interesting story about you."

Taken from How to Help Your Hurting Friend by Susie Shellenberger
Copyright © 2003 by Youth Specialties. Used by permission of Zondervan. www.zondervan.com.

1 incident – something that happens, especially something unusual or unpleasant

1. **Summarize** what the short story is about.

2. **Explain** how GoTo123 manages to gain Shannon's trust and to find out her identity.

3. You have a choice here. Choose **one** of the following tasks.

   a) *"Under 18-year-olds should be banned from social networks."*
   Comment on the statement from your point of view and include the following aspects:
   – reasons in favour of and against this statement
   – examples to support your arguments
   – what you do to keep safe on the internet

   or

   b) *"This man has just told us a most interesting story about you."*
   Write a suitable ending to the story and include the following aspects:
   – Shannon's reaction on seeing the stranger
   – the stranger's explanation
   – the parents' reaction
   – Shannon's explanation to the man's story
   – the agreement Shannon and her parents make for the future

Erster Prüfungsteil: Hörverstehen – Leseverstehen

Mittlerer Schulabschluss – Haupttermin

Wichtige Hinweise: Alle Texte, die im Folgenden zu hören sind, werden zweimal vorgespielt. Vor dem ersten Hören wird Zeit gegeben, sich mit den Aufgaben vertraut zu machen. Der Hörverstehenstest besteht aus zwei Teilen.

---

1 Hörverstehen Teil 1: *Racing to help*

---

*Together with her guest Dr. Michael Ryan, Mae Holland of CBC Radio Canada is presenting a historical race with a hero called Balto. First read the tasks. Then listen to the interview. While you are listening, tick the correct box **or** write down the information needed. At the end you will hear the interview again. Now read the tasks. You have **90 seconds** to do this.*
Now listen to the interview and do the tasks.

---

1 RADIO SIGNAL: "Nome calling … Nome calling … We have an outbreak of diphtheria … Urgently need help …"

MAE: On January 20, 1925, an urgent radio signal went out from Nome, a small town in Alaska. A local doctor had diagnosed diphtheria, an extremely catch-
5 ing disease of the throat and lungs. Lots of children in Nome had already died. The only hope to save the village was a special medicine – a serum – that was nearly 700 miles away. And this was not the only problem that needed to be solved, was it, Michael?

M. RYAN: Not at all. Winter in Alaska can be extremely dangerous, and there
10 was a heavy snow storm. The best way of getting the life-saving medicine to Nome in time was by plane. However, the only plane in the territory was on a flight to the lower part of the continent and therefore not available.

MAE: So something had to be done, and fast. Right?

M. RYAN: Exactly. Without the serum, hundreds of lives in Nome were in dan-
15 ger. So it was decided that a Pony Express-style team of 20 dog teams would take the extremely risky route. But before they could head off, the serum was first transported by train from Anchorage to Nenana, where the serum run started on January 27 with the first team.

MAE: I see. And so it happened that a dog called Balto rose to fame? What's his
20 story?

M. RYAN: Balto was the lead sleigh dog of the Norwegian Gunnar Kaasen's team of 7 dogs. Together they covered the last two parts of the dangerous trip to Nome. Balto was generally not thought of as a particularly good dog leader. Contrary to expectations, however, Balto fearlessly pushed ahead into
25 the ice-cold winds.

MAE: And Balto saved lives more than one time, right?

M. RYAN: Hell yes, he did. Visibility was near zero due to extremely heavy snowfall. Kaasen and his dogs had no route points, no orientation at all. But Balto was able to keep the team safely on the trail and even stopped them in time
30 before they could fall into certain death in the icy Topkok river.

MAE: Wow. What else threatened their mission?

M. RYAN: At one point, the winds were so bad that they actually lifted the sleigh AND dogs off the ground and the serum fell into the snow. Kaasen thought all was lost, but thankfully he was able to find the serum buried in the ice.
35 He, Balto, and his 6 teammates raced forward and arrived safely in Nome on February 2, 1925. The serum was handed over …

MAE: … and the town was saved.

M. RYAN: Right.

MAE: Balto still enjoys celebrity status today, doesn't he?
40 M. RYAN: He sure does. He became famous overnight. To honor his bravery and success, a statue of him was erected in New York's Central Park. Balto was the guest of honour. But sadly, his star soon began to fade. After a rough time he and his six teammates found a new home at a zoo.

MAE: To learn more about Balto and the great serum race, stay tuned …
45 [fade out]

Now listen to the interview again and check your answers.

1. a) … a serious illness.
   ✔ *Hinweis: "On January 20, 1925, an urgent radio signal went out from Nome, a small town in Alaska. A local doctor had diagnosed diphtheria, an extremely catching disease of the throat and lungs." (Z. 3–5)*

2. c) … the only plane was far away.
   ✔ *Hinweis: "However, the only plane in the territory was on a flight to the lower part of the continent and therefore not available." (Z. 11/12)*

3. c) … send sleighdogs.
   ✔ *Hinweis: "So it was decided that a Pony Express-style team of 20 dog teams would take the extremely risky route." (Z. 15/16)*

4. a) … to everybody's surprise.
    Hinweis: "*Balto was generally not thought of as a particularly good dog leader. Contrary to expectations, however, Balto fearlessly pushed ahead into the ice-cold winds.*" (Z. 23–25)

5. a) (there was) heavy snowfall / no visibility / no orientation / (there were) no route points
    Hinweis: "*Visibility was near zero due to extremely heavy snowfall. Kaasen and his dogs had no route points, no orientation at all.*" (Z. 27/28)

    b) (they) nearly fell into a river / (there were) bad winds / the sleigh and dogs were lifted off the ground
    Hinweis: "*But Balto was able to keep the team safely on the trail and even stopped them in time before they could fall into certain death in the icy Topkok river.*" (Z. 28–30); "*At one point, the winds were so bad that they actually lifted the sleigh AND dogs off the ground …*" (Z. 32/33)

6. b) … they almost lost the serum.
    Hinweis: "*… the serum fell into the snow. Kaasen thought all was lost, but thankfully he was able to find the serum buried in the ice.*" (Z. 33/34)

7. c) was invited to New York.
    Hinweis: "*To honor his bravery and success, a statue of him was erected in New York's Central Park. Balto was the guest of honour.*" (Z. 40–42)

8. c) … a challenge against time
    Hinweis: "*… something had to be done, and fast.*"(Z. 13);
    "*Without the serum, hundreds of lives in Nome were in danger. So it was decided that a Pony Express-style team of 20 dog teams would take the extremely risky route.*" (Z. 14–16);
    "*… the serum run …*" (Z. 17);
    "*… the great serum race …*" (Z. 44)

2   Hörverstehen Teil 2: *Easy money* by Gemma Ingram

> *You are going to hear a story about Stephanie who is worried about her grand-mother. First read the tasks. Then listen to the story. While you are listening, tick the correct box **or** write down the information needed. At the end you will hear the story again. Now read the tasks. You have **90 seconds** to do this.*
> *Now listen to the story and do the tasks.*

1   Stephanie was trying to explain to her grandmother how to record a television programme.

"Oh, I've got it now," said Gran. "This button is 'play'."

"No, that's 'stop'," said Stephanie.

5   "I must go, but I'll come back tomorrow and explain again."

That evening, Stephanie told Simon, "It's impossible. Gran loves new gadgets, but she can't work them! I explained how to record a programme three times this afternoon."

Next day, Stephanie stopped at her Gran's after work. She found her happily
10   watching a film from the day before. "Did you record that, Gran?"

"Oh, a nice young man has just moved into the house opposite. He did it for me."

"That's good," said Stephanie.

She thought, "Who is this man? Why does he want to help an old lady who
15   lives all alone?"

"You don't need to come every day, dear," Gran told Stephanie. "My young man will help me."

When Stephanie got into her car, she saw the young man opposite. His hair was long and his jeans had lots of holes.

20   "I'm worried," she told Simon. "Gran doesn't know this man. Maybe he'll try to take advantage of her."

"Or maybe he's just being nice," Simon replied.

"I'm going to find out."

A few days later, there was a bouquet of tulips on Gran's TV.

25   "Do you like the flowers my young man gave me? He's charming, but he needs his hair cut, it's too long."

"You don't give him money, Gran, do you?"

"Oh, just a few pence for programming the TV. I promised him a present if he gets his hair cut. He wants a car, but I don't know if they're expensive."

30   "Oh, no!" thought Stephanie. "Will you see him today?" she asked.

"Oh yes. He's coming at six for the John Wayne film."

As she left the house, Stephanie saw there were tulips in the garden next door. Some were missing.

She phoned Simon and explained, "You must come to Gran's at six. We must
meet him."

At ten to six, Stephanie arrived at her Gran's.

"Hi, it's Stephanie and Simon."

"Oh, come in, dears."

"I brought some biscuits," said Stephanie. "I made too many."

"Come and meet my young man. He loves biscuits."

In the living room, in front of the TV, was a young man in jeans. He had short
blond hair and two front teeth missing. Stephanie decided he must be seven years
old.

"This is Daniel," said Gran. "Daniel, this is Stephanie and Simon."

"Hello," said Stephanie.

"Thank you, young man," said Gran. She handed him ten pence and one of
Stephanie's biscuits.

"He lives with his dad," explained Gran.

"I look after him while his dad is decorating the house."

Daniel took a red car from his pocket.

"So you bought the car," said Stephanie, laughing.

"Yes. It only cost 50p at the market, and his dad pays me two pounds an hour
to look after him. Easy money!"

© *http://storywrite.com/Gemma_Ingram*

Now listen to the story again and check your answers.

Ende des Hörverstehenstests.

1. a) … but mixes things up.
   Hinweis: "'Oh, I've got it now,' said Gran. 'This button is "play"'.
   'No, that's "stop",' said Stephanie." (Z. 3/4)
   "… 'Gran loves new gadgets, but she can't work them! …'" (Z. 6/7)

2. b) … is enjoying an "old" TV broadcast
   Hinweis: "She found her happily watching a film from the day before.
   'Did you record that, Gran?'" (Z. 9/10)

3. a) … and questions the stranger's honesty.
   Hinweis: "She thought, 'Who is this man? Why does he want to help an
   old lady who lives all alone?'" (Z. 14/15); "'I'm worried,' she told Simon.
   'Gran doesn't know this man. Maybe he'll try to take advantage of her.'"
   (Z. 20/21)

4. b) … makes a decision.
   Hinweis: "'I'm going to find out.'" (Z. 23)

5. a) the stranger gives granny flowers / granny gives the stranger money /
   granny has promised the stranger a present
   Hinweis: "'Do you like the flowers my young man gave me? …'" (Z. 25);
   "'You don't give him money, Gran, do you?' 'Oh, just a few pence for pro-
   gramming the TV. I promised him a present if he gets his hair cut …'"
   (Z. 27–29)

   b) the stranger wants a car / tulips are missing (from the garden next door)
   Hinweis: "'… He wants a car, but I don't know if they're expensive.'"
   (Z. 29); "As she left the house, Stephanie saw there were tulips in the garden
   next door. Some were missing." (Z. 32/33)

6. the stranger is a child / the stranger is only seven years old / the stranger is the
   neighbour's child / the car is a toy
   Hinweis: "In the living room, in front of the TV, was a young man in
   jeans … Stephanie decided he must be seven years old." (Z. 41–43);
   "'He lives with his dad,' explained Gran. 'I look after him while his dad is
   decorating the house.'" (Z. 48/49);
   "Daniel took a red car from his pocket. 'So you bought the car,' said
   Stephanie, laughing. 'Yes. It only cost 50p at the market …'" (Z. 50–52)

7. b) … granny earned money and got cheap help.
   Hinweis: "'… his dad pays me two pounds an hour to look after him.
   Easy money!'" (Z. 52/53); "'My young man will help me.'" (Z. 16/17)

3 Leseverstehen: *Harriet Tubman – Secret Agent*

1. b) … guided runaway slaves to liberty.
    "… people who helped runaway slaves to get to freedom …"
    ✓ *Hinweis: Z. 4/5*

2. true
    "Despite a reward on her head, she returned to the South …" /
    "… Harriet and her passengers had many close calls."
    ✓ *Hinweis: Z. 7–12*

3. a) was a creative thinker.
    "She did what she could to trick people." /
    "Harriet often took slaves away on a Saturday night." /
    "Sometimes she poured pepper on the trail to confuse the dogs …" /
    "Sometimes she didn't head north right away."
    ✓ *Hinweis: (Z. 13–20)*

4. true
    "… the pistol on her belt … was also a symbol to instruct slaves, making it
    clear that 'dead Negroes tell no tales'."
    ✓ *Hinweis: Z. 21–23*

5. false
    "… she did her fair share of those jobs." /
    "… she nursed the sick and wounded."
    ✓ *Hinweis: Z. 26–28*

6. b) … because she did not raise any suspicion.
    "Tubman was a short woman without special features who moved unnoticed
    through rebel territory."
    ✓ *Hinweis: Z. 29/30*

7. true
    "… Harriet continued to help blacks create new lives in freedom."
    ✓ *Hinweis: Z. 34*

8. a) … thanks to a profitable deal.
    "… Bradford shared the money she made from it with Harriet."
    ✓ *Hinweis: Z. 42/43*

9. b) … the cause of Harriet Tubman's death.
    "She died in 1913 from pneumonia."
    ✓ *Hinweis: Z. 48*

This could happen to you

4 Wortschatz: *CyberSafety 101: Tactics for teens and young adults*

1. spend/waste/lose/...

2. a) ... trust ...

3. check/inform yourself about/look up/...

4. a) ... an increased ...

5. use/choose/access/...

6. communicating/communication/staying in touch/chatting/socializing/ connecting/...

7. b) ... careful ...

8. give/lend/...

9. c) ... reduce ...

10. secure/strong/safe/different/various/complex/complicated/...

11. d) ... prevent ...

12. reduce/limit/think about/...

13. c) Stealing ...

5 Schreiben

Hinweis: Bei den Schreibaufgaben werden dir keine konkreten Vorgaben zur Länge deiner Texte gemacht. Als ungefähren Richtwert solltest du bei Aufgabe 1 mindestens 80 Wörter, bei Aufgabe 2 mindestens 100 Wörter und bei Aufgabe 3 mindestens 120 Wörter schreiben.
Wichtig ist, dass in deiner Lösung alle in der Aufgabenstellung genannten Aspekte enthalten sind. Am besten gehst du deinen Text zum Schluss noch einmal durch und hakst die einzelnen Elemente in Gedanken ab. Außerdem solltest du deine Lösung noch einmal auf sprachliche Fehler hin kontrollieren.

1. *Hinweis: Bei dieser Aufgabe musst du den Inhalt der vorgegebenen Geschichte kurz zusammenfassen. Als Einstieg solltest du zunächst den Titel und den Namen der Hauptfigur nennen und in einem Satz erklären, worum es in der Geschichte geht. Danach gehst du auf die wichtigsten Etappen im*

Handlungsverlauf ein – dass Shannon verfolgt wurde, dass sie regelmäßig mit einem Unbekannten chattet und dass dieser die persönlichen Informationen aus ihren Nachrichten benutzt, um ihre Schule und ihren Wohnort ausfindig zu machen.

The story "This could happen to you" is about a teenager called Shannon and her rather careless internet activities, which eventually get her in a difficult situation.

One day as Shannon is walking home from school, she hears footsteps behind her. After she has arrived home safely, she goes online, logs onto a chat room, and contacts her chat partner GoTo123. She tells him about the incident and about her softball match at school that day. GoTo123 uses the personal information Shannon gives away in her messages and online profile to find out where she goes to school and to observe her. At the end of the story, we see him waiting for Shannon in her home, talking to her parents.

121 words

2. ✎ **Hinweis:** *Bei dieser Aufgabe musst du auf zwei Aspekte eingehen: Zum einen sollst du erklären, wie GoTo123 das Vertrauen von Shannon gewinnt. Zum anderen sollst du darlegen, wie es ihm gelingt, ihre Identität herauszufinden. Lies dir die Geschichte zunächst noch einmal genau durch und markiere relevante Textstellen. Mache dir dann einige Notizen, bevor du mit dem Ausformulieren der Lösung beginnst.*

GoTo123 succeeds in winning Shannon's confidence by building up a personal relationship with her in a chat room on the internet. He shares her worries when she tells him that she was followed, but also tries to calm her down. In addition, he shows interest in her favourite sport, playing softball.

To find out Shannon's identity, GoTo123 uses different strategies: Firstly, he asks clever questions like, "What is your team called?". Secondly, he searches online for her profile. Thirdly, he appears at her school during a softball match and identifies her with the help of her shirt number. In the end, GoTo123 is able to follow Shannon home and talk to her parents.

113 words

3. a) ✎ **Hinweis:** *Bei dieser Aufgabe sollst du begründen, ob Jugendliche unter 18 Jahren deiner Meinung nach aus sozialen Netzwerken ausgeschlossen werden sollten.*

Formuliere zunächst einen Einleitungssatz, in dem du auf das Thema hinführst. Gehe dann auf Argumente für und gegen ein Verbot von sozialen Netzwerken für Minderjährige ein und belege deine Aussagen mit Beispielen. Nutze beim Schreiben, falls nötig, die Formulierungen aus Aufgabe 4 (Wortschatz: CyberSafety 101). Sie können eine gute Hilfe sein.

Zum Schluss solltest du noch einmal deine eigene Meinung zum Thema zusammenfassen, und darlegen, was du persönlich unternimmst, um dich im Internet zu schützen.

More and more teenagers have a Facebook account. Some people worry about this fact. They think that this is dangerous and that for their own safety, under 18-year-olds should not be allowed to use social networks.

On the one hand, there are good reasons for banning minors from social platforms. Many young people are not aware of the risks when they go online. For example, they give away very personal information in their profiles – any person who might seem to be a friend could use this data for cyberbullying. In addition, future employers might see embarrassing posts or photos and then decide not to give that person a job.

On the other hand, social networks can also be very useful for young people. Facebook, Twitter etc. can be a great tool to get information, communicate with friends, or simply help each other with homework.

All in all, I think that under-18s should not be banned from social networks. However, they should get more information on how to communicate online safely. Many of the problems mentioned above can be avoided if certain basic rules are kept: For example, I post very little personal information, I use a nickname instead of my real name, and my profile can only be seen by my closest friends. In short, I try to keep safe on the internet by following the saying: Better to be safe than sorry!   *233 words*

b) ✎ *Hinweis: Bei dieser Aufgabe musst du einen passenden Schluss für die Geschichte schreiben. Du sollst darauf eingehen, wie Shannon und ihre Eltern auf den ungebetenen Besuch des Mannes reagieren, welche Gründe dieser für sein aufdringliches Verhalten nennt, und welche Vereinbarung Shannon am Ende mit ihren Eltern trifft.*
Lies dir die Geschichte zunächst noch einmal durch und überlege, welche Verhaltensweise zu den Figuren passen würde. Mache dir Notizen. Sieh dir dann genauer an, in welchem Stil der Text geschrieben ist. Die Geschichte ist in der dritten Person Singular und im „Past tense" gehalten. Gegen Ende des vorgegebenen Ausschnitts enthält sie außerdem einige Dialogpassagen. Deine Fortsetzung sollte in demselben Stil geschrieben sein – idealerweise sollte man keinen „Bruch" zwischen dem vorgegebenen Textausschnitt und deinem Schluss bemerken.

Shannon felt very confused and didn't know what to say. All she could do was stare at the man on the sofa.

"Dad, what's happening here? This man watched me during the game today. He must have followed me home … What is he doing in our house?" Her confusion now turned to anger. "I don't know you – get out of here!"

"Calm down, darling. Mr. Smith would like to tell you something," her father said.

Mr. Smith started explaining who he was. "My name is John Smith and I'm the father of your classmate Nancy. My daughter did the same as you – she gave away too much information about herself in a chat room. After a while she was stalked by a stranger, but luckily we found out. When I checked the conversations in the chat room I saw that you and my daughter had been writing to each other and that you had both been chatting with strangers. I decided to show you the danger of doing such a thing by making contact with you – first in the chat room, later at the sports ground and now here at your home."

Shannon was speechless.

Her father looked at her with a worried expression.

"Shannon, your mom and I were really shocked about what Mr. Smith told us. You really have to be more careful who you are chatting with and what you are telling them – this time, it's 'only' Mr. Smith, next time it could be God-knows-who … We're worried about you!"

Now tears started running down Shannon's face. "I'm sorry … I didn't … I wasn't … I often felt so lonely after school, and GoTo123 sounded like such a nice guy, like someone who really understands me …"

"Darling, you have to promise us that you won't chat with strangers again, no matter how nice they sound. And you know that you can always talk to us, your mom and me, when you are feeling sad or lonely, okay?"

"Okay, I promise. Right now, I'm not sure if I want to be ByAngel213 ever again …"

350 words

Erster Prüfungsteil: Hörverstehen – Leseverstehen

1 Hörverstehen Teil 1: *Mama Africa*

Penny Vale from BCC radio regularly chats with people
about topics and people that should not be forgotten.
With the help of today's guest Dorothy Masuku, Penny
Vale remembers the famous South African musician
Miriam Makeba.

- *First read the tasks.*
- *Then listen to the interview.*
- *While you are listening, tick the correct box.*
- *At the end you will hear the interview again.*
- *Now read the tasks. You have **90 seconds** to do this.*
- *Now listen to the interview and do the tasks.*

1. Miriam gained international celebrity …
   a) ☐ after a long career.
   b) ☒ thanks to a TV broadcast.
   c) ☐ with a hit in her home country.

2. Miriam Makeba spent her early life …
   a) ☒ in prison.
   b) ☒ without her mother.
   c) ☐ in a family of alcoholics.

3. Miriam's great voice was recognized by …
   a) ☐ her musical family.
   b) ☒ a South African band.
   c) ☐ two American relatives.

4. Miriam's musical style is …
   a) ☐ African-American.
   b) ☒ typically South African.
   c) ☐ a mixture of different influences.

5. Miriam got foreign attention through …
   a) ☒ a politically critical film.
   b) ☐ her production of an illegal film.
   c) ☐ her leading part in a film on Apartheid.

6. Because of her success in the US, Miriam …
   a) ☐ wanted to stay in America.
   b) ☐ was declared a criminal outcast.
   c) ☒ lost permission to enter her country.

7. Miriam got her nickname "Mama Africa" …
   a) ☐ for her life as a singer.
   b) ☐ for her sacrifice to South Africa.
   c) ☒ for her work as a pioneer and role model.

8. Later, the US let Makeba down because of her …
   a) ☒ relationship with a political rebel.
   b) ☐ political views concerning South Africa.
   c) ☐ commitment in American political affairs.

9. Miriam Makeba died …
   a) ☐ in US exile.
   b) ☒ as a free woman.
   c) ☐ after a long illness.

2 Hörverstehen Teil 2: *Mamohato Children's Centre* 🔊

Prince Harry, who lost his mother at a very young age, opened a children's care centre during his South African tour in 2015. Listen to his opening speech.

- *First read the tasks.*
- *Then listen to the speech.*
- *While you are listening, tick the correct box or write down the information needed.*
- *At the end you will hear the speech again.*
- *Now read the tasks. You have* **90 seconds** *to do this.*
- *Now listen to the speech and do the tasks.*

1. When Prince Harry first came to Africa he …
   a) ☒ realised the needs of the children.
   b) ☐ saw how independent the children were.
   c) ☐ was shocked by the high rate of youth crime.

2. Harry points out that he and the children …
   a) ☒ suffered the same fate.
   b) ☐ had people to help them.
   c) ☐ knew that time would heal.

3. When Prince Harry saw the children in 2004 he …
   a) ☐ helped at once.
   b) ☒ wanted to help fast.
   c) ☐ wondered when to help.

4. Back then, Prince Harry already …
   a) ☐ saw the lack of money.
   b) ☐ asked volunteers to sign up.
   c) ☐ wished for more local support.

5. Today's scientific reports show that …
   a) ☐ HIV children suffer from loneliness.
   b) ☐ infected children need better medicine.
   c) ☐ people are more open-minded towards sick people.

6. At the centre children learn how to live with their illness.
   Give **two** examples.
   a) _____
   b) _____

7. The charity organisation Sentebale has …
   a) ☐ organised medical exams.
   b) ☐ built new homes for families.
   c) ☐ spent hours talking to politicians.

8. Talking about challenges, Prince Harry states that …
   a) ☐ Mamohato has to learn about HIV.
   b) ☐ most African teenagers die of HIV.
   c) ☐ Africa is important in fighting HIV.

New, Multiracial Beginning in Story of "Madam & Eve"
John Murphy (Baltimore Sun)

JOHANNESBURG, South Africa – The doorbell rings at the home of Madam Gwen, but Eve, the black maid, refuses to answer it. Madam reluctantly pulls herself up from the sofa and opens the door. "I don't think I've ever seen you answer the door before," says the startled[1] visitor, a neighbor.

5 "I wouldn't let Eve have time off to see her Uncle Joe, so now she's getting back at me," says Madam. "By making you answer the door?"

"Forget about the door. She's protesting by not doing her work. She's on a go-slow."

10 "A go-slow? How slow is she going to go?" Eve enters from the kitchen, walking at an exaggeratedly slow pace as if her feet are stuck in glue. She delivers tea to a displeased Madam and her guest. "Well, at least she made you tea," says the visitor.

15 "I asked her last night," Madam says wryly[2].

So goes the first episode of "Madam & Eve," a popular South African sitcom to hit television screens. Based on a popular comic strip of the same name, "Madam & Eve" explores the awkward relationship between a wealthy white woman and her black maid as they try to make their way in post-apartheid South Africa.

20   Signs of political and social change are everywhere in the new South Africa, but there are few places like television to understand how South Africans see themselves – or would like to see themselves. Under Apartheid, a show such as "Madam & Eve" would have had no chance of getting on the air. But since the democratic elections in 1994, television producers are turning to multiracial sitcoms as 25 an entertaining way to deal with the country's uncomfortable past and perhaps show a path to the future. South Africans want to look at South African life comically. They like to laugh at themselves. But behind the laughter, "Madam & Eve" delivers its share of social commentary.

Sitcoms are allowed to play with cultural stereotypes, such as the rich madam, 30 the poor maid, the old racist Afrikaner and the Zulu grandmother, freeing the show's writers and viewers to explore the contradictions and complexities of South Africa today.

What sets South African television apart from its American and British counterparts is that by law, all shows must include as many of the country's 11 official 35 languages as possible.

To an outsider, it makes for strange, often confusing, viewing. In "Madam & Eve," for instance, Eve speaks Zulu with the family's black gardener but will talk

with the Madam in English. Sometimes viewers are provided subtitles; other times, viewers are expected to understand the conversation within context or with repeti-
40 tion.

Some critics view the visual humor – the funny faces, the objects falling on people's heads and toes – as a way of reaching across a multilingual audience.

Fearing that it would be a dangerous, perhaps revolutionary technology, television was banned by Apartheid leaders until 1976, when the first government-
45 owned station, the South African Broadcasting Corp., went on the air with tightly controlled news, sports and entertainment programs.

Early on, a black person could not appear in the same frame as a white person. Half of the programs were in English and half were in Afrikaans. Native African languages were rarely heard. But over the years, the restrictions were relaxed some-
50 what as the government launched two more stations broadcasting in black tribal languages.

In 1994, South African television was liberated from its Apartheid restrictions. Viewers now have their choice of the state-run South African Broadcasting Corp.'s three channels with programming in all 11 languages, independent e-TV[3] and sev-
55 eral pay channels with home-grown shows. American, British and other foreign imports make up nearly half of all shows on television. Audiences, however, still prefer anything made in South Africa, because the shows reflect their own experiences.

Text: http://articles.latimes.com/2001/mar/07/entertainment/ca-34178
Illustrationen: © Stephen Francis & Rico, www.madamandeve.co.za

1 startled – here: confused, surprised
2 wryly – showing that you are both amused and disappointed or annoyed
3 e-TV – South Africa's biggest independent TV channel

"Madam & Eve" is based around the theme of a middle-class white woman and her black maid. Theirs is a relationship of friendly quarrelling.

• *Tick the correct box **and** give evidence from the text.*

---

1. The introductory scene of *Madam & Eve* is funny because …
   a) ☒ the maid is on strike.
   b) ☐ a stranger opens the door.
   c) ☐ Madam treats her guest rudely.
   Evidence from the text:
   (Z.5.) Forgot about the door.

2. The storyline of *Madam & Eve* was invented for a TV series.
This statement is … ☐ true ☒ false
Evidence from the text:

Based on a popular comicstrip (L.17)

3. TV is seen as a good way to reflect on South African identity.
This statement is … ☐ true ☐ false
Evidence from the text:

_____

4. Today's South African TV productions …
a) ☐ limit satirical programmes.
b) ☐ treat Apartheid with humor.
c) ☐ favour sensitive over funny broadcasts.
Evidence from the text:

_____

5. Shows like *Madam & Eve* work with clichés to help understand South Africa.
This statement is … ☐ true ☐ false
Evidence from the text:

_____

6. South African TV must represent several African languages.
This statement is … ☐ true ☐ false
Evidence from the text:

_____

7. During Apartheid, watching TV was restricted because of …
a) ☐ poor financial resources.
b) ☐ outdated technical equipment.
c) ☐ concerns about bad influences.
Evidence from the text:

_____

8. Discrimination on TV showed in the underrepresentation of …
a) ☐ black people.
b) ☐ African languages.
c) ☐ native programmes.
Evidence from the text:

_____

9. Today, South African viewers give priority to international TV imports.
This statement is … ☐ true ☐ false
Evidence from the text:

Zweiter Prüfungsteil: Wortschatz – Schreiben

"The Gun"

4 Wortschatz: *"A South African experience"*

Michelle Faul and her mixed-race family experienced racist incidents in South Africa in the early 60s, forcing them to leave the country for England. Today Michelle Faul is Chief Africa correspondent for "The Associated Press". She looks back at what life was like in South Africa during Apartheid.

> • *Fill in suitable words or tick the correct box.*

1. My widowed mother had driven us from our _____ in Zimbabwe, which was then called Rhodesia, to visit family in her native South Africa.

2. There was racism in Rhodesia, too, but it was nothing like the laws in South Africa that made blacks subhuman because they had to …
   a) ☐ suffer   b) ☐ hurt
   c) ☐ experience   d) ☐ feel
   in the most horrible ways.

3. We did not take the train because halfway through the trip, passengers would have to get out of the Rhodesian Railway compartment and _____ _____ to old and run-down black-only South African carriages.

4. The car trip presented its own challenges. Hotels _____ only whites and everywhere you could see signs declaring places and facilities "for whites only".

5. Only whites were allowed inside the stores. So we had to carry piles of food and drinks from home because our mother _____ to go to the back door of shops.

6. Being white meant you could live where you wanted. However, …
   a) ☐ circles of   b) ☐ crowds of
   c) ☐ cliques of   d) ☐ clouds of
   blacks were caged in townships, if they could get jobs in the city.

7. If they didn't get jobs, their urban shacks – poor homes – were _____
   _____ so that black South Africans had nowhere to live. They
   were then moved by force to unproductive "homelands".

8. My experience was more of absurd trivialities of Apartheid, rather than
   brutal …
   a) ☐ attack   b) ☐ strike
   c) ☐ violence   d) ☐ storm
   used to uphold it.

9. If you were white, you had …
   a) ☐ access to   b) ☐ entrance to
   c) ☐ arrival to   d) ☐ reception to
   jobs denied to blacks.

10. The only black professionals were teachers, like my mother, lawyers like
    Mandela and nurses and doctors, who could only _____
    black patients.

11. My mother spoke English. But to guarantee white superiority even at school,
    black learners should be taught to speak Afrikaans, the _____
    of the Apartheid regime.

12. Today, South Africa is a democratic country where everybody has the right
    to …
    a) ☐ choose   b) ☐ elect
    c) ☐ vote   d) ☐ select
    so that their voices may be heard.

13. It is a tribute to Mandela's efforts that today, I and others forgive but do not …
    a) ☐ forget.   b) ☐ lose.
    c) ☐ remember.   d) ☐ suppress.

5 Schreiben

The gun *by Beverly Naidoo*

*Esi and his parents are faithful and valued employees at the Mackay game farm[1]
at the time of the South African Apartheid regime. When their boss Mackay has to
leave one day, he asks his future son-in-law Williams to take charge until Mackay's
return.*

Early the following afternoon, there was the familiar sound of Mackay's Land Rover entering the camp. Esi saw immediately that it was being driven by the young man Williams – and he was alone. When he jumped down from the driver's seat, he was carrying Mackay's gun. Although he could only be a few years older than
5 Esi, there was something in his manner that reminded Esi of the sneering[2] officer in the Mapoteng[3] attack. His bush-green eyes narrowed on their target.

"What're you staring at? You've seen me before, haven't you? Go get your boss-boy[4] for me. Be quick about it, jong[5]!"

Esi could feel his face going hot, but he turned rapidly and sprinted off. Even
10 Mackay never spoke to him like that, always calling him by his name.

Esi accompanied his father as he walked forward to greet the white man. He wanted to see how Papa would react.

"You remember me? ... Boss Williams. Boss Mackay has asked me to come and look after his place, so we better get on, you and me. I don't want any trouble
15 from the other boys either, OK?" He turned to Esi.

"You can get my bags out the back and carry them to my room." Papa simply gave a little nod. It was impossible to tell what he was thinking. His lined face remained quite passive as father and son carried the young white man's cases.

Before long it was clear that Williams assumed Esi to be his personal servant.
20 Up till now Esi had taken instructions either from his father or Mackay, who had known him since he was little. But this man's manner was different. He didn't seem to care at all who Esi was. It was as if he was just a thing to be used.

Much of the time Williams would sit on the veranda outside Mackay's room, legs stretched out on a stool, a can of beer at his side, while cleaning or playing
25 with Mackay's gun.

"Hey, come clean my boots!"

"You can wash the truck now!"

"Make my bed properly, jong! Don't just pull the sheets up like that!"

"Do you call these boots clean? If you were in the army I'd donder[6] you! Do
30 them again!"

"Go call the girl! I want her to do my washing this morning."

At the last order, Esi had to fight to control himself. Who did this man think he was? Didn't he know that "the girl" was Esi's own mother, old enough to be

the white man's mother? When Esi found her, busy collecting wild spinach, his
35 anger spilled out.

She tried to calm him. His temper would get him into trouble. He should try to
be like his father. "Papa just lets them push him around. I don't want to be like
that!"

"Ha! What else can you do my young man?"

40 And with that his mother began walking slowly, steadily, toward the camp to
collect the dirty washing.

Text: Beverly Naidoo: Out of Bounds. Seven Stories of Conflict and Hope.
London: Puffin Books / Penguin 2001.

1 game farm – a farm with wild animals
2 sneering – unpleasant, arrogant
3 Mapoteng – a South African village
4 boss-boy – insulting expression for an adult man who is in charge of something
5 jong – expression from Afrikaans meaning 'boy'
6 donder – expression from Afrikaans meaning 'hit' or 'bully'

- *Read the tasks carefully.*
- *Make sure to write about **all** the aspects presented in each task.*

---

1. **Describe** Williams' behaviour towards Esi and his parents and how it com-
   pares to that of Boss Mackay.

2. **Explain** how Williams' behaviour is reflected in the language he uses and the
   reaction it causes in Esi.

3. You have a choice here. Choose **one** of the following tasks.

   a) Esi's mother tolerates Williams' behaviour and states: "What else can you
      do?"

      Comment on this statement and remember that this story is set during the
      Apartheid regime.

   or

   b) Esi cannot accept his mother's attitude. When Williams calls Esi again and
      bosses him around, Esi cannot control himself any longer. **Write down**
      how the story goes on.

      Include the following aspects:

      – Esi's reaction
      – William's reaction
      – the consequences for everybody

Lösungsvorschläge

Erster Prüfungsteil: Hörverstehen – Leseverstehen

Mittlerer Schulabschluss – Haupttermin

Wichtige Hinweise: Alle Texte, die im Folgenden zu hören sind, werden zweimal vorgespielt. Vor dem ersten Hören wird Zeit gegeben, sich mit den Aufgaben vertraut zu machen. Der Hörverstehenstest besteht aus zwei Teilen.

1   Hörverstehen Teil 1: *Mama Africa*

*Penny Vale from BCC radio regularly chats with people about topics and people that should not be forgotten. With the help of today's guest Dorothy Masuku, Penny Vale remembers the famous South African musician Miriam Makeba. First read the tasks. Then listen to the interview. While you are listening, tick the correct box. At the end you will hear the interview again. Now read the tasks. You have **90 seconds** to do this. Now listen to the interview and do the tasks.*

1 PENNY VALE: Today is part of our music month and I'll be using the BCC archives to take us back to 1959. And in the days when just arriving in the United States a young female singer from South Africa called Miriam Makeba was catapulted into stardom literally overnight.

5 MIRIAM MAKEBA: I did one song on the Steve Allan Show and that was it, because he had 60 million viewers.

PENNY VALE: Dorothy, tell us about the young Miriam.

DOROTHY MASUKU: Miriam Makeba's start in life in Johannesburg in 1932 was dramatic. It was hard for her father to get a job. And so her mother brewed

10 some beer. And it was illegal for Africans to drink alcohol at any time, and her mother was caught and she was arrested. Miriam Makeba was 18 days old and her mother spent 16 months in jail with her.

PENNY VALE: Oh no. How was Miriam's talent for singing discovered?

DOROTHY MASUKU: In Makeba's family there was always music. Her mum, her

15 grandmother, her sister and brother used to sing on Sundays and just get together and sing. Miriam got her big breakthrough when she was still a teenager after she was asked to sing with one of South Africa's most popular bands, the Manhattan Brothers. She went on to form the Skylarks, an all-woman group which sang a blend of jazz and traditional melodies of South Africa.

20 PENNY VALE: So how come she became an international star?

DOROTHY MASUKU: Miriam became known first outside South Africa after a small role in the film "Come back Africa". The film secretly exposed the brutalities of Apartheid and it was an instant hit.

PENNY VALE: But Miriam paid a high price for her fame abroad.

25 DOROTHY MASUKU: Mhm. A year after taking the US by storm she tried to return to South Africa but the Apartheid regime said no. Her mother died. It was then that she woke up to the fact that she couldn't come back home. Her papers were no longer valid.

Miriam had to spend 30 extraordinary years in exile. Miriam became known 30 affectionately as Mama Africa, not just because she was the first singer to take the melodies of Africa to the rest of the world, but also because she was a symbol of the struggle against Apartheid. In 1963 she even called for action against Apartheid before the United Nations.

PENNY VALE: But in 1968 the US establishment's love affair with Mama Africa 35 came to an abrupt end because of another love affair.

DOROTHY MASUKU: Mhm. Concerts and recording contracts were cancelled when she married Stokely Carmichael, a leading and controversial civil rights activist and a member of the Black Panthers. She didn't know why this was thrown at her. She wasn't involved in the politics of the United States. She'd simply 40 picked a man, not his politics. Only after the release of Nelson Mandela in 1994 was Mama Africa finally free to return to her homeland.

In 2008 Miriam Makeba died at the age of 76 doing what she most loved. She had just finished a concert with her signature tune "Pata Pata" when she suffered a heart attack as she came off stage.

Now listen to the interview again and check your answers.

---

1. b) … thanks to a TV broadcast.
   / *Hinweis: "I did one song on the Steve Allan Show and that was it …" (Z. 5)*

2. a) … in prison.
   / *Hinweis: "Miriam Makeba was 18 days old and her mother spent 16 months in jail with her." (Z. 11/12)*

3. b) … a South African band.
   / *Hinweis: "Miriam got her big breakthrough when she was still a teenager after she was asked to sing with one of South Africa's most popular bands, the Manhattan Brothers." (Z. 16–18)*

4. c) … a mixture of different influences.
   Hinweis: "She went on to form the Skylarks, an all-woman group which sang a blend of jazz and traditional melodies of South Africa." (Z. 18/19)

5. a) … a politically critical film.
   Hinweis: "Miriam became known … after a small role in the film 'Come Back Africa'. The film secretly exposed the brutalities of Apartheid and it was an instant hit." (Z. 21–23)

6. c) … lost permission to enter her country.
   Hinweis: "It was then that she woke up to the fact that she couldn't come back home." (Z. 26/27)

7. c) … for her work as a pioneer and role model.
   Hinweis: "Miriam became known affectionately as Mama Africa, not just because she was the first singer to take the melodies of Africa to the rest of the world, but also because she was a symbol of the struggle against Apartheid." (Z. 29–32)

8. a) … relationship with a political rebel.
   Hinweis: "Concerts and recording contracts were cancelled when she married Stokely Carmichael, a leading and controversial civil rights activist and a member of the Black Panthers." (Z. 36–38)

9. b) … as a free woman.
   Hinweis: "… in 1994 was Mama Africa finally free to return to her homeland. In 2008 Miriam Makeba died at the age of 76 …" (Z. 40–42)

> *Prince Harry, who lost his mother at a very young age, opened a children's care centre during his South African tour in 2015. Listen to his opening speech. First read the tasks. Then listen to the speech. While you are listening, tick the correct box or write down the information needed. At the end you will hear the speech again. Now read the tasks. You have **90 seconds** to do this.*
> *Now listen to the speech and do the tasks.*

1 "Eleven years ago I made my first visit to Lesotho, with the help of Prince Seeiso. I couldn't believe that so many children had been robbed of their childhoods by extreme poverty and the ravages of HIV and AIDS. Behind those smiles it was clear they desperately needed care, attention and above all, love.

5   Although our situations couldn't have been more different, I felt a strong connection to many of the children I met. They were far younger than me, and of course, their situation was a great deal more challenging than my own. But we shared a similar feeling of loss, having a loved one, in my case a parent, snatched away so suddenly. I, like them, knew there would always be a gaping hole which
10 could never be filled.

Experiencing this first hand in 2004 put all my experiences and worries into perspective. From that moment, it wasn't a question of when but how quickly we could put something in place which could help these children, robbed of the carefree childhood many other children across the world enjoy.

15   It was already obvious to me that a great deal of valuable work was being done by local people across these communities. But it was also clear that the volunteers and organisations weren't able to attract the financial support they needed. Prince Seeiso and I felt that we could make a meaningful and long-term difference to these children.

20   Research showed us that children living with HIV received little support to help them deal with the social and psychological challenges of their condition. As a result they felt isolated and afraid to face up to their illness.

The theory of our Mamohato camp is simple – if children have the chance to share with each other how HIV affects them and how they cope with it in a safe
25 and accepting environment, they will lead healthier, more well-adjusted lives. Through these camps, children learn about their condition and can then share this knowledge with their peers once they return home. HIV-focused games, sports, arts, crafts and drama all help to inform while boosting self-confidence.

This centre is now the heart of Sentebale; it represents how far we have come
30 as a charity but more importantly how much more we want to achieve.

Much has already been accomplished. Sentebale and its partners have provided care for 5,000 orphans, delivered 1/4 million hours of psychosocial support and, this year alone, tested 13,000 adults and children for HIV – 62 % of whom were women and girls.

35 Many countries face the challenge of HIV and AIDS, particularly across Southern Africa. In fact, according to UNAIDS, HIV remains the number 1 cause of death amongst adolescents in Africa. We hope the Mamohato Children's Centre will become a centre of excellence for the region; allowing us to share this valuable local knowledge and experience with partners in other countries.

Text: https://www.royal.uk/speech-prince-harry-official-opening-sentebales-mamohato-childrens-centre-lesotho (zu Prüfungszwecken gekürzt und adaptiert, nachgesprochen von Daniel Holzberg)

> *Now listen to the speech again and check your answers.*

> *Ende des Hörverstehenstests.*

1. a) … realised the needs of the children.
   ✏ *Hinweis: "Behind those smiles it was clear they desperately needed care, attention and above all, love." (Z. 3/4)*

2. a) … suffered the same fate.
   ✏ *Hinweis: "But we shared a similar feeling of loss, having a loved one, in my case a parent, snatched away so suddenly." (Z. 7–9)*

3. b) … wanted to help fast.
   ✏ *Hinweis: "From that moment, it wasn't a question of when but how quickly we could put something in place which could help these children …" (Z. 12/13)*

4. a) … saw the lack of money.
   ✏ *Hinweis: "But it was also clear that the volunteers and organisations weren't able to attract the financial support they needed." (Z. 16/17)*

5. a) … HIV children suffer from loneliness.
   ✏ *Hinweis: "As a result they felt isolated and afraid to face up to their illness." (Z. 21/22)*

6. learn about their condition / share this knowledge with their peers (when they return home) / HIV-focused games / sports / arts / crafts / drama / boost self-confidence
   ✏ *Hinweis: "Through these camps, children learn about their condition and can then share this knowledge with their peers once they return home. HIV-focused games, sports, arts, crafts and drama all help to inform while boosting self-confidence." (Z. 26–28)*

7. a) ... organised medical exams.
   Hinweis: "*Sentebale and its partners have ... tested 13,000 adults and children for HIV ...*" *(Z. 31–33)*

8. b) ... most African teenagers die of HIV.
   Hinweis: "*In fact, according to UNAIDS, HIV remains the number 1 cause of death amongst adolescents in Africa.*" *(Z. 36/37)*

3 Leseverstehen: *New, Multiracial Beginning in Story of "Madam & Eve"*

1. a) ... the maid is on strike.
   "She's protesting by not doing her work. She's on a go-slow."
   Hinweis: Z. 8/9

2. false
   "Based on a popular comic strip of the same name, 'Madame & Eve' explores ..."
   Hinweis: Z. 17/18

3. true
   "... there are few places like television to understand how South Africans see themselves – or would like to see themselves."
   Hinweis: Z. 21/22

4. b) ... treat Apartheid with humor.
   "... since the democratic elections in 1994, television producers are turning to multiracial sitcoms as an entertaining way to deal with the country's uncomfortable past ..."
   Hinweis: Z. 23–25

5. true
   "Sitcoms are allowed to play with cultural stereotypes, such as the rich madam, the poor maid, the old racist Afrikaner and the Zulu grandmother, freeing the show's writers and viewers to explore the contradictions and complexities of South Africa today."
   Hinweis: Z. 29–32

6. true
   "... by law, all shows must include as many of the country's 11 official languages as possible."
   Hinweis: Z. 34/35

7. c) ... concerns about bad influences.
"Fearing that it would be a dangerous, perhaps revolutionary technology, television was banned by Apartheid leaders until 1976 ..."
⟡ *Hinweis: Z. 43/44*

8. b) ... African languages.
"Native African languages were rarely heard."
⟡ *Hinweis: Z. 48/49*

9. false
"Audiences, however, still prefer anything made in South Africa ..."
⟡ *Hinweis: Z. 56/57*

Zweiter Prüfungsteil: Wortschatz – Schreiben

"The Gun"

4   Wortschatz: *"A South African experience"*

1. home / house / ...

2. a) ... suffer ...

3. change / move / transfer / switch / ...

4. accepted / welcomed / allowed / served / accommodated / ...

5. did not want / refused / ...

6. b) ... crowds of ...

7. destroyed / knocked down / bulldozed / ruined / demolished / ...

8. c) ... violence ...

9. a) ... access to ...

10. treat / help / take care of / ...

11. language / tongue / ...

12. c) ... vote ...

13. a) ... forget.

5 Schreiben

✎ Hinweis: Der Prüfungsteil „Schreiben" besteht aus drei Aufgaben. Mit der ersten Aufgabe wird überprüft, ob du den Ausgangstext verstanden hast. Die zweite Aufgabe geht bereits etwas tiefer – hier musst du auch auf die im Text verwendete Sprache eingehen. Bei der dritten Aufgabe hast du die Wahl zwischen einer persönlichen Stellungnahme oder einer kreativen Aufgabe. Überlege, welche der beiden Aufgaben (3a oder 3b) dir besser liegt und beginne dann zügig mit der Bearbeitung.

1. *✎ Hinweis: Lies dir den Text bezüglich der Aufgabenstellung gut durch und mache dir gegebenenfalls entsprechende Notizen. Wichtig ist bei dieser Aufgabe, dass du Williams' Verhalten gegenüber Esi und seinen Eltern beschreibst (Wie benimmt er sich ihnen gegenüber? Was sagt er zu ihnen?) – du brauchst also keine persönliche Wertung abzugeben. Danach vergleichst du dieses Verhalten mit den Informationen, die du im Text zum Verhalten von Mackay erhältst. Schreibe mindestens 80 Wörter.*

Williams' behaviour can be described as racist. From the beginning, he treats Esi and his parents, who are black, as servants without any rights. He orders Esi to do all kinds of chores, while he himself relaxes on the veranda. His behaviour towards Esi's parents is similarly humiliating – although they are much older than him, he constantly bosses them around. Williams seems to feel totally superior as a white man. He further underlines his position of power by provokingly playing around with a gun.

In contrast to this, the behaviour of Mackay is much more respectful. For him, Esi and his parents are employees whom he appreciates, not just servants or "objects" to be used at will. This is also evidenced in the simple fact that he calls them by their names rather than just "girl" or "boy".   *138 words*

2. *✎ Hinweis: Hier ist es deine Aufgabe, zu erklären, inwieweit sich Williams' Verhalten in seiner Sprache widerspiegelt und welche Reaktionen dies bei Esi auslöst. Lies dir den Text in Hinblick auf diese Aspekte erneut durch, unterstreiche die entsprechenden Stellen oder mache dir Notizen. Deine Lösung sollte mindestens 100 Wörter umfassen.*

Williams' racist attitude is also reflected in his language. Instead of calling Esi and his parents by their names, Williams uses derogative expressions like "girl", "boy" or the Afrikaans word "jong". This is particularly degrading for Esi's parents who are much older than Williams but are thus made to feel like children. In addition, almost all of Williams' sentences are made up of imperatives which he uses to order Esi and his parents around (rather than asking them politely to do something).

For Esi, Williams' way of talking to them – or rather down at them – is very humiliating. He feels increasingly angry – both with Williams, for treating them so badly and with his parents, who don't seem to say or do anything against Williams' racist behaviour.   *126 words*

3. a) ✒ ***Hinweis:*** *Bei dieser Aufgabe musst du eine persönliche Stellungnahme zum Zitat von Esis Mutter schreiben. Ihre Frage "What else can you do?" drückt aus, dass weder sie noch ihr Mann eine Möglichkeit sehen, sich gegen Williams' respektloses Verhalten zu wehren. Du sollst nun begründen, ob du diese Ansicht teilst oder nicht. Dabei ist es wichtig, dass du auch auf die Situation in Südafrika während der Apartheid eingehst, da die Geschichte nur vor diesem Hintergrund zu verstehen ist.*
Mache dir zunächst Notizen zu den Argumenten, die für oder gegen die Haltung von Esis Mutter sprechen. Beginne erst dann mit dem Ausformulieren deiner Lösung. Als Einleitung solltest du das Zitat von Esis Mutter kurz in den Zusammenhang der Erzählung einordnen. Im Hauptteil wägst du die Argumente gegeneinander ab. Zu guter Letzt solltest du knapp zusammenfassen, inwieweit du mit der Äußerung von Esis Mutter übereinstimmst. Insgesamt sollte deine Lösung mindestens 120 Wörter umfassen.

In Beverly Naidoo's story "The Gun", Esi is disappointed because his parents seem to tolerate the racist behaviour of "Boss" Williams. His mother's question "What else can you do?" expresses her resignation to the situation. But is there really nothing one can do or is Esi right when he expects them to rebel?

In order to answer this question one has to consider the context in which the story is set. During the time of Apartheid, black people were oppressed and denied even basic human rights. Rebelling against that injustice meant risking your life or being thrown into prison – Nelson Mandela, for example, spent 27 years in jail. In this context, it is understandable that Esi's mother does not want to get into conflict with Williams or the authorities – the danger of being severely punished or torn apart as a family was simply too high.

On the other hand, I can see why Esi is not satisfied with his parents' reaction. If everyone acted like that and if no one stood up for their rights, nothing would ever change. People like Mandela paid a high personal price when they fought against the Apartheid system. However, they succeeded in bringing about change for the whole of society: The system of Apartheid was finally abolished and black people were given equal rights.

The question of how to behave in the face of injustice is not an easy one to answer. The behaviour of Esi's parents, who are merely trying to protect their family, is understandable. However, history has shown that only the selfless and courageous fight of individuals like Nelson Mandela was able to bring about freedom and civil rights to all people in South Africa.

284 words

b) **✎ Hinweis:** *Bei dieser Aufgabe geht es darum, die Erzählung möglichst nahtlos fortzusetzen. Achte darauf, dass dein Text zum bisherigen Handlungsverlauf der Geschichte passt und in derselben Perspektive (3. Person Singular) und Zeitstufe („past tense") geschrieben ist. Da der Ausgangstext Dialoge enthält, sollte deine Fortsetzung ebenfalls entsprechende Passagen beinhalten. Außerdem solltest du beim Verfassen des Textes die Situation in Südafrika während der Apartheid berücksichtigen.*

Mache dir zunächst Notizen, bevor du mit dem Ausformulieren deiner Fortsetzung beginnst. Überprüfe dabei auch noch einmal, dass du wirklich auf alle in der Aufgabenstellung genannten Aspekte eingehst (Esis Verhalten, Williams' Reaktion und die Konsequenzen für alle Beteiligten). Schreibe mindestens 120 Wörter.

Esi tried to follow his mother's advice and stayed away from the camp and Williams for a while. But an hour later he was ordered back to get further instructions from Williams.

When he arrived he saw his mother on her knees, collecting clothes from the ground. Williams, with the gun in his hand, was yelling at her: "Girl, is that supposed to be clean? Do it again! And you, *jong*, bring me another beer!"

Unable to hold back his anger, Esi ran towards Williams and beat him to the ground. He took the gun that Williams had lost during the attack and pointed at him. "Don't call my mother 'girl'! One more word and I ... I ...!"

Williams, totally surprised by the attack, tried to get back to his feet. "Boy, you don't know what you're doing. This will have serious consequences ...!" Esi, still pointing the gun at Williams, felt a growing insecurity in his body when he saw his mother crying and looking at him. He threw the gun away and tried to flee, but stumbled over a piece of wood. Williams, taking up the gun again, shouted harshly: "I told you, *jong*! Get yourself into the car, NOW! We'll see what the police thinks about boys who don't know their place!"

At the police station Esi was questioned by two officers. They asked him how he could dare to beat his boss and point a gun at him, too. Esi replied with a strong voice: "Williams isn't my boss, it's Mackay!" One officer got very angry and beat him. They grabbed Esi and threw him in a tiny cell.

It was already dawning when the cell door finally opened and Esi saw Mackay waiting outside. "Get into my car, you foolish young man!"

Back at the farm, Mackay took Esi to his office. Williams was already sitting here, staring at the floor. Mackay started to speak with a strong voice. "I can't believe what has happened in my absence. I'm very disappointed with both of you. Now listen to me – there'll be no more guns on this farm. And both of you will have to pay for your behaviour. You'll get extra work to do! But before that you must apologise to each other."

Williams and Esi shook hands, not looking at each other.

"Now, get out of my office and start working." *398 words*